How to Use your Reading in your Essays

Palgrave Study Skills

Business Degree Success
Career Skills
Cite Them Right (9th edn)
Critical Thinking Skills (2nd edn)
e-Learning Skills (2nd edn)
The Exam Skills Handbook (2nd edn)
The Graduate Career Book
Great Ways to Learn Anatomy and Physiology
How to Begin Studying English Literature (3rd edn)
How to Manage Your Distance and Open
    Learning Course
How to Manage Your Postgraduate Course
How to Study Foreign Languages
How to Study Linguistics (2nd edn)
How to Use Your Reading in Your Essays (2nd edn)
How to Write Better Essays (3rd edn)
How to Write Your Undergraduate Dissertation
Improve Your Grammar
Information Skills
The International Student Handbook
IT Skills for Successful Study
The Mature Student's Guide to Writing (3rd edn)
The Mature Student's Handbook
The Palgrave Student Planner
Practical Criticism
Presentation Skills for Students (2nd edn)
The Principles of Writing in Psychology
Professional Writing (2nd edn)
Researching Online
Skills for Success (2nd edn)
The Student's Guide to Writing (3rd edn)
The Student Phrase Book
Study Skills Connected
The Study Skills Handbook (4th edn)
Study Skills for International Postgraduates
Study Skills for Speakers of English as a Second
    Language
Studying History (3rd edn)
Studying Law (3rd edn)
Studying Modern Drama (2nd edn)
Studying Psychology (2nd edn)
Teaching Study Skills and Supporting Learning
The Student Phrase Book
The Undergraduate Research Handbook
The Work-Based Learning Student Handbook
Work Placements – A Survival Guide for Students
Write it Right (2nd edn)
Writing for Engineers (3rd edn)
Writing for Law
Writing for Nursing and Midwifery Students
    (2nd edn)
You2Uni

Pocket Study Skills

14 Days to Exam Success
Blogs, Wikis, Podcasts and More
Brilliant Writing Tips for Students
Completing Your PhD
Doing Research
Getting Critical
Planning Your Essay
Planning Your PhD
Reading and Making Notes
Referencing and Understanding Plagiarism
Reflective Writing
Report Writing
Science Study Skills
Studying with Dyslexia
Success in Groupwork
Time Management
Writing for University

Palgrave Research Skills

Authoring a PhD
Getting to Grips with Doctoral Research
The Foundations of Research (2nd edn)
The Good Supervisor (2nd edn)
The Postgraduate Research Handbook (2nd edn)
Structuring Your Research Thesis

How to Use your Reading in your Essays

Second edition

Jeanne Godfrey

First published 2013 by
PALGRAVE MACMILLAN

Palgrave Macmillan in the UK is an imprint of Macmillan Publishers Limited, registered in England, company number 785998, of Houndmills, Basingstoke, Hampshire RG21 6XS.

Palgrave Macmillan in the US is a division of St Martin's Press LLC, 175 Fifth Avenue, New York, NY 10010.

Palgrave Macmillan is the global academic imprint of the above companies and has companies and representatives throughout the world.

Palgrave® and Macmillan® are registered trademarks in the United States, the United Kingdom, Europe and other countries

ISBN: 978–1–137–29468–5

This book is printed on paper suitable for recycling and made from fully managed and sustained forest sources. Logging, pulping and manufacturing processes are expected to conform to the environmental regulations of the country of origin.

A catalogue record for this book is available from the British Library.

A catalog record for this book is available from the Library of Congress.

For my family

Contents

Acknowledgements

This second edition, as in the first, is a product of the knowledge and experience I have gained over the years. I would, therefore, like to thank all the students I have taught, and colleagues and other experts in the field whose work I have read, discussed and pondered as I progress in my own understanding. I would also like to thank again the Palgrave Macmillan team for their support in bringing this second edition to publication, especially Suzannah Burywood, Della Oliver and Alec McAulay.

Introduction: an example and overview of how reading is used in an essay

A fundamental part of academic study is reading other people's work on a subject and using what you have read to develop your own thinking and writing. This book will take you through the process of using what you read in your written work, from deciding what to read to checking your work for mistakes. *How to Use your Reading in your Essays* looks specifically at using your reading in non-exam essays, but the information it gives is also relevant to most types of academic writing across most subject areas. This book will increase your knowledge of how to use the chapters, books and articles you read effectively, and will thereby give you the confidence to produce good writing and to get the highest marks possible for your work.

This book will show you:

- how to decide which types of books and articles are suitable to read for your essays and which are probably not;
- how to understand and question what you read;
- what information to write down and how to make notes that enable you to use your reading properly and effectively in your essays;
- why, when and how to use quotations in your essays;
- why, when and how to put what you read into your own words;
- why, when and how to integrate your own points with ideas from your reading;
- words and phrases to use when you are integrating and evaluating your reading;
- brief explanations of grammatical areas that often cause problems in student writing;
- examples of common mistakes to check for and to avoid in your own work.

How to Use your Reading in your Essays takes you through the process of using your reading in clear stages, and gives you key points, examples and practice exercises, using real texts and student essays. It explains simply and clearly both the 'why' of using your reading and the practical 'how' of doing so.

In Part A of this second edition I have included some short extracts from my book *Reading and Making Notes*, 2010. These are the sections on using your university library, reading methods, and points for making notes. In Part B (sections B2 to B5) I have included some adapted material from my book *The Student Phrase Book*, 2013.

The rest of this introductory section gives you an example and overview of how reading is used in a non-exam essay and gives you points to remember when you are writing your own assignments.

An example and overview of how to use your reading in an essay

Below is a section of an excellent undergraduate short essay. At university you will be given different types of assignments on a variety of topics, but the style of writing in this essay will be common to many of them. We will look at different sections of this essay throughout this book and you will find the complete essay in Appendix 3, pp. 144–48.

Look at the essay sections and notice how the student has used the books and articles he has read (referred to as sources) in his essay. The essay sections are colour-coded to help you do this.

Black = student   student's own knowledge, ideas and words.

Blue = source   information and ideas from what the student has read,
                         using either the exact words from the source (a quotation)
                         or his own words (a paraphrase or summary).

Red   = in-essay reference   information that indicates when a source has been used
                         and who the author is.

Outline what business ethics is and discuss whether it is important. (2,000 words)

Over the past couple of decades, the ethical credentials of businesses appear to have become an explicit factor in consumer choice. An illustration of this is the current number of publications in the UK that give consumers information on what are called 'ethical companies'. The Ethical Company Organisation (2012) for example, lists businesses ranging from pet food producers and florists to banks and stationery companies, and the organisation offers companies 'ethical accreditation'. The UK ethical market is valued at over 30 billion euros per year, and there are currently over 14,000 books and 4 million web entries related to business ethics (The Co-operative Bank 2008, cited in Crane and Matten 2010). In this essay I will first describe what business ethics is and will then consider whether it is important as a concept and as an aspect of business activity.

There are numerous, overlapping definitions of business ethics. Shaw and Barry (2007) define it as 'the study of what constitutes right and wrong (or good and bad) human conduct in a business context' (p. 25). Another definition describes business ethics as the 'principles and standards that guide behaviour in the world of business' (Ferrell et al. 2002 p. 6). It is important to emphasise here that business ethics is not synonymous with legality. There is some overlap between law and ethics, but legislation usually only regulates the lowest level of acceptable behaviour (Crane and Matten 2010). In addition, as Trevino and Nelson (2010) point out, the law is limited in

Annotations in right margin:

- Student point
- Sources used as evidence and support for student point
- Student aims
- Student point
- Sources used as support
- Student point
- Sources used as support

what it can do to prevent unacceptable actions, because legislation follows rather than precedes trends in behaviour. **Business ethics then, as** Crane and Matten **state,** is mainly concerned with areas of conduct that are *not* specifically covered by law and that are therefore open to different interpretations, a fact that means a particular behaviour may be legal albeit viewed as unethical.

> Sources used as support

Another important distinction to make is that ethics is not equivalent to general morality. Crane and Matten **explain that** although morals are a basic premise of ethics, ethics and ethical theory go a step further because they focus on how morals can be *applied* to produce explicit standards and rules for particular contexts, of which business is one. **I define business ethics here then, as any aspect of business standards and/or behaviour that directly or indirectly relates to moral principles. Importantly, an action can be considered ethical regardless of whether it arises from a genuine desire to be moral or merely as a result of profit-driven motives.**

> Student point

> Sources used as support

> Student definition and student point

et al. = and the other authors.

Comments on how the student has used his reading in his essay

The student's own points (shown in black)

In the essay the student gives five of his own points, his own definition and states clearly his aim (he chooses not to give a firm view of which he will try to persuade his reader, also called a thesis statement). Throughout his essay the student first introduces his own point and then uses what he has read (his sources) as evidence and support for the point he is making. He then gives a final comment on his point and/or moves on to his next point. You can see this 'wrapping' pattern clearly in the essay extract by looking at the colour sequence, particularly in the first and third paragraph – black, blue, black.

Use of sources (shown in blue)

Note that the student uses only two short quotations, and these are the definitions given in the second paragraph. His complete essay uses a total of only six short quotations; most of the time the student puts the sources into his own words.

Use of in-essay references (shown in red)

Every time the student uses a source he gives it an in-essay reference (sometimes called an in-text reference or citation). He does this not only when he uses a quotation but also when he puts a source into his own words. These in-essay references make clear to the reader which ideas and comments are his, and which ones come from his reading.

The student has used an author and date (year) system of referencing, and this system will be used throughout this book. The other main way of referencing is to use a sequence of numbers and corresponding footnotes, called a numeric system. Examples of common referencing styles are given in Appendix 4, pp. 149–151

Five key points to remember when you are writing an essay

1 **Preparing and writing an essay at university involves three main processes:**
   - reading the work of others to help develop your own knowledge and thoughts on a subject;
   - using what you have read to help develop your own ideas, argument and answer to the essay title;
   - expressing what you have read in your own words, showing how your reading relates to your own points.

2 **Don't be afraid of using sources and *showing* that you have used them**
   Your tutors will expect your essay to use several or perhaps many different sources, and to show when you have used them. Don't worry that doing this will make your essay seem unoriginal. Your essay will still be your own piece of work because of the choices you make in selecting which sources to use, the way you express what they say in your own words, and how you use your sources to develop your own argument and your own individual answer to the essay title.

3 **Every time you use words and/or ideas from your reading, use an in-essay reference**
   References make clear to the reader what you have read in order to help develop your own thinking, and how you have used your reading to develop your own argument and answer to the essay question; this is good scholarship and will gain you marks. In addition, if you do not give in-essay references your tutor will not be able to see which parts of the essay are your own points, and so you may not get the marks you deserve for your research. You must also always give references each time you use a source in order to avoid accidentally representing ideas from your reading as your own.

4 **Put your reading into your own words as often as possible**
   Using your own words shows that you have understood what you have read and also allows you to rework, control and use your reading to support your own points. It is the only way to develop your own ideas and to get good marks, and is also the key to the good written communication skills that employers look for in graduates.

5 **Using your reading properly in your writing takes time and practice**
   Even professional writers can find writing very difficult. Good writing takes time and practice, and integrating your reading into your own writing is a very complex skill. Your tutors will expect you to develop these writing skills gradually, and do not want your essays to be over-complicated or full of long words. They want to see writing that is clear and well thought through, and the key to this is to give enough time to all three parts of the writing process: reading, thinking and writing.

Using your reading

Introduction to Part A: key points for reading at university

The types of books and articles you read at university will probably be different from those you used at school or college. Why and how you read at university will also be different, requiring more independence from you in deciding what to read, higher levels of concentration and more questioning of the material. Finally, as you will have seen from the main introduction, the way in which reading is used in academic essays makes this type of writing quite different from work you may have done up to now.

Part A gives you:

- important information and strategies to take you through the process of reading and of using this reading in your essays in the form of quotation, paraphrase or summary;
- real academic articles, real student writing and an excellent short student essay to demonstrate each stage of the process;
  short practice exercises on all of the points covered.

It is best to go through each section of Part A in order, but you can also read and re-read different sections as and when you need.

Five key points to remember about reading

- A common reason why students struggle with reading at university is simply that they do not give enough time to it, and so don't enjoy it because of the stress of trying to fit too much reading into too little time. Reading and thinking is where most of your learning and creativity will happen, so take it seriously and make reading a priority in your time management schedule.
- Identify your purpose for reading a book or article and decide what it is you want to learn from it, and then be flexible in how you read, matching your reading method to your reading purpose. You may need to read some articles from start to finish, but for other texts you may only need to scan briefly or read just one particular paragraph in detail.
- Try to engage with the material rather than just reading the words on the page. This means being (or becoming) interested in what you are reading, and thinking about what the author is doing and trying to say. This will greatly improve your understanding and will further increase your interest in the subject.
- Some of the books and articles you need to read may seem complex, formal and difficult to understand at first. Everyone approaches reading in a slightly different way and it may take

a little time to build up your 'reading muscles' and to discover what works best for you. Start by reading short articles or short sections before tackling longer ones; as with everything else, you will improve with practice. Bear in mind that most people need to re-read complex texts, and that the struggle to understand is a normal part of taking in new information.

- Reading will also help improve your writing skills by increasing your knowledge of new words and your awareness of how to structure a piece of written work. Bear in mind however, that not everything you read will be well written.

How do you decide what to read?

It seems obvious that for a good essay you need good sources, but what exactly *is* a 'good' source? When looking for sources, don't be tempted to just type your essay title straight into an online search engine in the hope that something useful will come up. Knowing what types of sources are suitable for university work, and spending some time thinking about what information you need before you start searching, will save you a great deal of time and will result in a much better piece of work. This section gives you the key steps and information you need for finding the best sources for your essay.

Five steps for deciding what to read

Step 1 Think: what question do you want to answer?

Do some thinking before you start searching for sources. Check that you really understand the title of your essay. For example, does the title ask you to develop an argument, give your opinion, give examples, or some of these things together? Does it ask for definitions, information on a process, advantages and disadvantages or for different views on an issue?

Rewrite the title in your own words – this will really help you to understand it. For example, the business ethics essay title could be rewritten as: 'Give a brief overview of what business ethics is and then argue that business ethics either is or is not important, giving your reasons for your view'.

Step 2 Think: what do you already know about the topic and what ideas do you already have?

Think (and perhaps write down) what you already know and think about the essay question. For the business ethics essay, you would ask yourself what *you* think business ethics is and whether *you* think it is important. You will probably also have already have done some reading and discussion on the essay topic during your course, so think about what you have already read that is relevant.

Step 3 Think: what types of source will you need?

Make notes on any suggested reading and other instructions about sources your tutor has given you. Think about what types of sources you will need to answer your essay title.

For example, which of the following will you need?

- an introductory textbook to give you some initial ideas;
- chapters in more advanced textbooks;
- important major works on the topic;
- original data from experiments or other research;
- recent academic journal articles on new developments or ideas on the topic;
- non-expert or public opinion on the issue.

For the business ethics essay, after thinking about the essay title, the student decided to look in some current academic textbooks for definitions of business ethics. He also read some relevant journal articles and reports by key authors for their views on the importance of business ethics, and he also decided to look at some company websites to find out what businesses themselves say about business ethics.

Step 4   Do a first search

Decide how good you want your essay to be and how much time and effort you are willing to give to finding appropriate sources. Then use your thoughts on the types of sources you need to start searching. Looking for sources is called a literature search, and it is a vital part of academic research. As you search, keep checking that your sources are relevant, specific and reliable (see below).

Content pages and chapter headings of books and journal article abstracts can help you to decide whether a source is relevant. Reading the introduction and conclusion of a book chapter or journal article is also a quick way of finding out whether a source will be useful. The reference list at the end of one book or article may provide you with details of further useful sources.

It is important at this stage to write down the precise details of each source you think you might use (author, date, title, journal/publisher) and also where and how you found it. You may not think this is important but you will be surprised how useful this information is, and remember that for academic work, *who* wrote something is as important as what they wrote about.

Is it better to use the library or to do your own online search?

With so much material available online, some students don't go near their university library until the end of their second year or later. This is a real shame because your library can help you with some of the very problems that arise from information overload. Don't make the mistake of thinking that the internet is just like a big online library – it isn't!

Searching for sources using the university library

Advantages
- Material has already been pre-selected by lecturers and library staff for its importance, relevance, reliability and academic quality.
- The intranet and library catalogue material (again, chosen by your tutors/library) are more likely to be reliable than material from the internet.
- Library staff are there to help you with selecting and finding texts.
- Has an online catalogue system that contains all its resources. Will also give you free access to other academic online databases.

- You can use the 'sort' facility of the library catalogue to put sources in order of publication.
- Has primary printed material and back copies of journals, newspapers and magazines that are not available online.
- Has specialist dictionaries, study guides and material written by your university not available online (e.g. advice on how to reference your work).
- Provides a quiet and comfortable environment in which to study, away from distractions.
- Has free Wi-Fi connection and use of DVDs
- Has free use of magazines and newspapers, dictionaries, encyclopaedias and other print material.
- Will probably have agreement with other libraries.

Disadvantages
- The copies of a book or article may be out on loan (but you can reserve them!).

Searching for sources using the internet

Advantages
- A huge number of sources are available.
- 24 hour access every day of the year (although your library may also be open 24 hours a day).

Disadvantages
- Search engines will often return a large number of returns and false matches, and so it can be hard to find the most relevant source.
- It is sometimes difficult to find out who wrote something and whether the source is reliable and peer-reviewed.
- A significant number of academic sources are not yet available online.
- You often have to pay for downloads of complete books or articles.

Step 5 Think, sort and select your sources for detailed reading

When you have done your first search for sources, think again about what you will want to say in your essay and what you think your conclusion might be. This may change as you read more, but by now you should have some idea of how you want to answer the essay title.

You might need to do some general background reading on a topic, but most essay titles will ask for something specific, so try not to waste time by reading sources that are on the correct general topic but that are not specific enough. For the business ethics essay, you would not want to spend time reading about general business topics or about the meaning or history of ethics; you would need to focus specifically on *business* ethics. Even when you had found a book on business ethics, you would not need to read it all, just the chapters or sections which described what business ethics is and whether/why it is important.

Select your sources for more detailed reading and ask yourself the following questions about each source.

- What type of source is it and who wrote it?
- Is it relevant and specific to my essay?
- Is it a reliable and academic source?
- Why exactly am I going to read it?
- Will it probably support my conclusion or give an opposing viewpoint?
- Will I probably use it as an important piece of information or only as a minor source?

What is a reliable source?

At university you are expected to make sure that your sources are reliable – that you can trust what they say. This usually means knowing who wrote something and that they are an authority on their topic. Reliable sources are usually those that have a named author, as this ensures that you reader knows who is accountable for the information given. Anonymous sources are much more likely to be of poor quality and/or contain incorrect information.

Up-to-date information will probably be more reliable than older information, so check when your source was written. You may want to read older sources that are key texts or to build up your knowledge, but for most topics you will also need current sources. Always check online sources to see when they were last updated and whether any links are active.

A reliable source is also one that gives information that is as accurate and complete as possible, rather than giving only the information that suits the author's purpose. Business and political organisations for example, may present information in a biased way. However, you need to think about what 'reliable' means for the type of information you need. If your essay is about public opinion in the media, then newspapers and television programmes would be a reliable source for this particular type of information. Equally, if you are writing about the views of different political organisations, their leaflets and websites would provide reliable information on what these views are, even though such information may not be balanced or reliable in the general sense of the word.

Are abstracts, reviews and summaries reliable sources?

These are all useful in different ways to give you a general idea of a text, but are not reliable sources in themselves as they do not give enough detail.

Article abstracts

Written by the author. Abstracts give an outline of the argument but not always the conclusion. You will not be able to evaluate the evidence, argument or conclusion of the article fully just by reading the abstract.

Summaries of a book or article

Could be written by the author or by someone else. A summary does not provide enough detail for you to be able to evaluate the evidence or argument of the source.

Article or book reviews

Always written by someone else. If the review has been written by an expert, it may give you useful information about the context of the source and other published work in the field. However, reviews are of no use for detailed information and may often be the biased, personal opinion of the reviewer.

Introduction and conclusion of a book or article

Written by the author. Reading just the introduction and conclusion of a source will give you a good idea of the main points and argument, but are not enough for you to evaluate the evidence or argument of the whole article, section or book.

Primary and secondary sources

Try to find the original (primary) source of information where possible, as something that is reported second or third hand may not be accurate and will be relatively unreliable. If you want data on the results of an experiment, try to read the original report rather than use an article that discusses the experiment second-hand (this is called a secondary source). Similarly, if you want to write about what an expert has said, read the actual book or article they have written rather than an article by another author who discusses what the expert has said. In reality, it will not always be possible or necessary to use only primary sources, but your tutor will usually expect you to read the key primary sources on a topic.

For the business ethics essay, the student found some primary material about companies from their websites. The textbooks and articles he used were partly primary material but they also discussed the previous work of other experts and so also acted as secondary sources of the material they used. Several of the articles mentioned a key text written by Albert Carr in 1968, so the student made sure that he found and read this primary source.

What is an academic source?

For most university assignments you will need to use information from sources that are not only reliable but are also regarded as academic. Academic sources are those written by authorities on a topic and which have usually been peer-reviewed. The peer-review process is when the book or article is sent by the publisher to other experts for checking and discussion before being published. Peer-reviewed sources are reliable, and are called academic (or reputable or authoritative) sources because they have been written by people who have attained a high standard of knowledge and research in their subject. Reliable and academic sources always have a named author or organisation. The academic community relies on knowing who wrote what, so that academics in a particular field can question, discuss and work with each other to build knowledge and develop ideas.

Non-academic sources

Below is a list of source types which are not academic and should not normally be used as sources for university essays:

- encyclopedias (including Wikipedia, which is an online encylopedia);
- college-level textbooks;
- newspapers (including long articles in quality papers such as *The Times* or *The Guardian*);
- magazines (including quality magazines such as *The Economist, Newsweek* and *New Scientist*);
- news or TV Channel websites (e.g. the BBC News);
- trade publications and company websites;
- publications and websites of charities, campaign or pressure groups;
- student theses or essays;
- pamphlets and brochures;
- blogs and wikis.

Checking that your sources are academic

Books and journals on the library shelves and on your reading lists will usually be reliable and academic. However, you may want to find other sources, and you will need to make the effort to check that these are also reliable and academic. Books have normally gone through a peer-review process and so are usually reliable. Journals described as an academic journal, a peer-reviewed journal or a scholarly journal will be reliable and academic.

Check your online sources

Take particular care when you are using online sources. Your tutor will suggest suitable places to search online but it is your responsibility to check that your sources are reliable and academic. Wikipedia may be useful for some initial definitions and to give you links to other sources, but you should not use it as an actual source in your essay. This is because Wikipedia is a type of encyclopedia and is therefore only a basic summary and a secondary source. It is also anonymous and is not peer-reviewed and is therefore not reliable and not academic.

Words that should warn you that an online article is probably not academic are: *magazine, digest, personals, news, press release, correspondent, journalist, special report, company, classified, personals and advertisement.* However, don't be fooled into thinking that an online article is reliable and academic just because it is well-written and has an author's name, includes statistics and has in-text references. Even words such as *journal, research or volume/issue number, Society or Research Centre* are being increasingly used by unreliable and non-academic sources and websites. You need to check that the article is in fact from a peer-reviewed journal.

Check your online databases

Some online databases contain only peer-reviewed academic journals, but some of them (even one which describes itself as a 'research database') also contain newspapers, magazines and trade publications. Read the description of the database before you go into it – what does it say it contains? You may be able to google a database and get a description of its publications from the 'home' or 'about us' page.

Remember – always check whether an article is academically reliable, even if you have found it through a database.

Check your web search engines

Search engines such as Google, Yahoo and Bing are not usually appropriate or helpful when searching for academic sources. Google Scholar is better, as it contains only literature related to academic work, but you still need to be careful, as not all of this literature is peer-reviewed material – Google Scholar also includes some magazines and student theses.

Where to check a website

If you are not sure about the reliability of an online website, article, database or search engine, try to find its homepage and look under sections such as 'about us' 'contact us' 'editorial board' 'board of directors' 'information for authors' 'submission process' 'sponsors' 'funders' and 'partners'. These sections will give you information about who runs and supports the website, and whether its articles are peer-reviewed.

Practice 1: would you use these sources?

Read the descriptions below of ten potential sources for five different essay titles. Do you think these sources are not reliable, reliable but not academic, or reliable *and* academic?

Sources for an essay on government support for people with disabilities
1   An article written in July 2006 in an online magazine called 'Mobility Now'. It has news, information and stories and is a magazine for people with disabilities. It is published by a leading charity organisation for people with disabilities.

Sources for an essay on youth crime
2   A recent online article on ASBOs written by Jane Smith, Home Correspondent. The URL is the online business section of a national quality newspaper.

Sources for an essay on recent developments in stem cell research
3   An online article on stem cells, published jointly by three authors in 2009. The article has a date, volume and issue number. The article on a website called 'Stem Cells'. This seems to be the title of the journal and at the bottom of the page there is a publisher: Beta Res Press. In the 'information for authors' section, the website tells authors how to track the progress of their article as it goes through the peer-review process.
4   Three different online science publications with similar titles that all look like magazines. They all have news sections, advertisements and jobs sections. They all have issue numbers and two of them also have volume numbers.
   4a   The first one has an 'about us' page that describes how its correspondents get their information by contacting leading scientists, reading scientific journals and websites and attending conferences.
   4b   The second magazine has the name of an organisation at the top of its website. On its 'about' page it describes the magazine as its journal, and states that it is a peer-reviewed

general science journal. Another page states that its board of directors consists of university academics.

4c   The third publication has no 'about us' information. Wikipedia describes the magazine as 'a well-respected publication despite not being peer-reviewed'.

Sources for an essay on developments in animal cloning

5 An article from a printed booklet titled 'Animal Cloning' published in 1999. There is a series of booklets, each with a volume and issue number. Each booklet contains a collection of short articles and newspaper and magazine clippings which give a simple introduction to issues and public debate on a scientific topic.

Sources for an essay on business ethics

6 A well-written report (which starts with an executive summary) on business ethics in companies. The website is run by an organisation called SEB – Social Ethics in Business. On the 'about' page, the organisation describes itself as part of a network of business organisations that focus on corporate responsibility. Its funders and partners are large national and international business foundations and development agencies.

7 An online article titled 'Business Ethics Guidelines'. The website address is 'Harold Jones International Company'.

8 An online article about McDonald's on a website called 'Centre for Management Research'. There is no 'about us' page but there is a homepage stating that the centre is involved in business research, management consulting and the development of case studies and training materials.

9 An online article on business ethics found on the website of the 'Centre for Business Ethics' of a university. On the centre's homepage it states that it helps businesses and the community, and offers workshops, conferences and lectures. It also states that the centre publishes its own *Journal of Ethics*.

10 An online article about a drinks company's activities in India. The article has no author but is well written and says 'for immediate release' at the top of the page. The website is titled as a 'Resource Centre'. The 'home /about us' page states that the centre has evolved from networks and discussions by activists, and describes itself as a platform for movements to publicise their demands and apply pressure to governments.

(*The articles and websites are fictitious but are closely based on real examples*).

How do you understand and question what you read?

When you sit down to read a book, chapter or article (we can call all of these *texts*) you should usually already know what type of text it is, who wrote it, that it is reliable and academic, and that it is relevant and specific to your essay question, so you will probably already have some idea about its content. The next step is to sit down and actually read it. This may sound straightforward, but the two most common reasons for students getting low marks for their essays are firstly, not reading carefully enough and/or not properly understanding the main point of the text, and secondly, not questioning what they read.

To use your sources effectively you need to really understand each text, and to read it with some questions in mind. This section gives you advice, examples and practice for doing so.

Five steps to understanding and questioning what you read

Step 1 Think: why are you reading?

Before you start reading a text, ask yourself *why* you are going to read it and what type of information you are looking for. For example;

- Are you looking for the answers to specific questions (e.g., what business ethics is or whether it is important)?
- Are you looking for general information on a point that you don't know much about and that will help you develop your own ideas and argument?
- Are you just looking for just a few basic facts, or do you need to read in detail so that you can follow the author's argument?
- Are you looking for evidence and examples as support for what you want to argue in your essay?
- Are you looking for points which you will then argue against?
- Look at who wrote the text and at the title and sub-titles, and make some predictions about what the text might say. It doesn't matter if your predictions turn out to be wrong – the important thing is to get engaged and interested in what you are going to read.

Step 2 Match your reading method to your reading purpose

In reality there simply isn't enough time to read everything from cover to cover, and you probably wouldn't want to anyway. We read different things in different ways, and you should apply the same principle to your academic reading – matching the *way* you read something to *why* you are reading it.

Three different ways to read

Scanning – looking over material quite quickly in order to pick out specific information
You might scan when you are browsing a database for texts on a specific topic, or you might scan a text for specific information. You might also scan when you are looking back over material to check something.

Gist reading – reading something fairly quickly in order to get the general idea
You might do this by reading just the headings, introduction and conclusion, or you might read for gist by going over the whole text fairly quickly. You might want to read for gist in order to decide whether to reject a text or to go back and read it in more detail. Reading for gist is also sometimes called 'skimming' or 'reading for breadth'.

Close reading – reading something in detail
You may want to read something in detail for several different reasons: as background reading; as a 'way in' to a new and difficult topic; to make sure you understand discussions of data, or to clearly understand the detail or argument. Close reading is also called 'reading for depth'.

It is important to remember that scanning or reading for gist is *not* a substitute for close reading. You will need to do a lot of detailed reading for academic work and the whole point of only scanning or gist reading some texts is to give you enough time for careful and close reading of the more important ones. You need, therefore, to develop the skill of recognising when it is appropriate to scan, when to read for gist and when to do close, careful and reflective reading.

Remember also to stay flexible about which reading method to use. You will often need to use combinations of methods, not just across different texts but also within a single text – zooming in and out. You might, for example, first quickly read over a whole text for gist, then read a section of it in detail, read some bits you find difficult again *very* carefully, and finally go back and scan the text for anything you think you may have missed.

You might also decide to change your reading approach as you read. After reading a quarter or a third of the text, ask yourself 'Is it giving me what I want? Am I learning and thinking as I read? Do I understand what I'm reading?' If the answer to these questions is no, then stop and think about why this is. It may be that you dived straight in with close reading and that it would be better to zoom out and get the general feel of the text first before going back to the detail. It may be that you need to find an easier text as a way in to the topic, or it may be that the material is not as relevant as you thought and that you should stop and move on to something else.

Step 3 Read actively

Read with your questions in mind. If you are only looking for one or two facts, you can just quickly scan the text for this information. Usually however, you will want to read in more detail. It may be better *not* to write anything down at this stage. Read the first section of the text (or all of a short text) and try to identify:

- what the key message of the text is;
- which parts of the text are main points, which are more minor points and which parts are examples of the points made;
- which parts of the text are facts, which are description and which are the author's opinion.

Try to identify what the author is trying to do overall. For example, are they giving information, putting forward an idea or theory, arguing and trying to persuade you of something, or a combination of these things? Finally, explain to yourself what the main point of the text is in your own words.

Step 4 Read, ask questions and evaluate

Read the text again and this time, question, evaluate and locate what the author says, using the prompts below (you can do this either in your head or on paper).

Question what the author says

- What assumptions does the author make?
- Do you think these assumptions are correct?
- Are the stages of the argument clear and logical?
- Does the conclusion follow from the evidence given?
- How does the author's argument and position fit in with what you already know?

Evaluate what the author says

- Are you persuaded by what the author says? Why/why not?
- If someone asked your opinion of the author's viewpoint, what would you say?
- Stand back and give the text an overall evaluation:
  what is the author's general way of thinking and position on the issue?
  what are they trying to do and how well do they do it?
  why do you think people would read this text, and do *you* think it is worth reading?
  how you think your background, experiences and viewpoint have affected what you think about the text?
- How has the text developed, modified or perhaps completely changed your thinking and therefore your argument?
- How will you use what the author says in your argument?

Step 5 Locate the author, other authors and yourself in the subject area

Locate the author in the subject area

- Find out who the author is and who they work for (Internet search engines are useful for this).

- Does the author's argument belong to a particular school of thought (e.g. behaviourism, Marxism, feminism)?
- How is the author's argument different or similar to other experts on the subject?

Locate other authors and yourself in the subject area

After reflecting on the specific text you have read, relate it to the other material you have read on the topic. As you do more reading, try to build up a mental picture of the 'location' of different authors.

- How do different texts you have read on the subject differ and how are they similar?
- Where does each author sit in the subject?
- Which authors agree with each other and which disagree?
- Are there any authors who have a unique position?

Think about where you now sit in the subject area, and which authors are closest to your own current position.

Opinion, critical analysis and argument

Students often think (or are told) that they should not give their opinions in an essay. It is true that you should not just give your personal opinion about something based only on your feelings. However, you *are* expected to give your opinion on an issue or essay question, provided that you have arrived at it through clear reasoning. Your reasons should be supported by evidence, and you should come to a conclusion that is persuasive because it follows logically from your reasoning and evidence. This sequence is called an argument. Arguing in academic study does not mean that you have to argue *against* something; an argument in the academic sense means a logical, structured and evidenced answer or conclusion to an issue or question.

As part of your argument, you will need to state whether you agree or disagree with the sources you discuss, and you won't be able to do this unless you have analysed (broken down), questioned, evaluated and located them, as shown above. The analysis involved in this process is sometimes called 'critical analysis', and the whole process is part of what is called a 'critical thinking approach'. As with the word *argument*, critical thinking in the academic sense does not mean that you can only say negative things about a text; indeed, you might want to be very positive about it. Critically analysing a text just means that you have asked yourself questions about what it says and formed your own views on it, based on clear reasoning rather than just personal experience or opinion.

Looking at an example of questioning, evaluating and locating a text

Below are three short sections from a long article the student read for his business ethics essay. Read the extracts to give you some idea of the authors' argument, and then look at the student's informal notes showing his thoughts from his critical analysis of the whole article.

A Model of Business Ethics

If one searches the literature, it appears that in the thirty years that business ethics has been a discipline in its own right a model of business ethics has not been proffered. This paper attempts to address this gap in the literature by proposing a model of business ethics that the authors hope will stimulate debate (see Figure 1). This model is one that is predicated on the tenets of developed countries operating within a capitalist paradigm.

. . .

Socially responsible managers do the right thing because it is the right thing to do. It is the correct action to take and an action that society expects. Executives should "act ethically not out of fear of being caught when doing wrong. Rather, they should embrace ethical behaviour in business because of the freedom, self-confirmation, and success that it brings" (Thomas et al., 2004, p. 64).

. . . it is important to see business ethics as a highly dynamic and continuous process without an end. A process, however, that is predicated on the interrelationship between business and society where each one is interdependent and responsible together for the outcomes. Hoffman and Moore (1982) suggest that the pre-eminence of business ethics is because of a perceived failing, by the general community, of business to act for the general good of the society. They, therefore, suggest that the mutual obligations of business to the community and the community to business need to be restated.

Extracts from: Svensson, G. and Wood, G. (2008) 'A model of business ethics' *Journal of Business Ethics*, 77, pp. 303–322.

The student's thoughts on the Svensson and Wood article

Questioning

The authors look at businesses operating in a developed world, capitalist context. Presumably there are lots of businesses outside these types of context – how do they behave? Svensson and Wood also seem to assume that individuals and society always expect businesses to behave well and to trust them – I don't think they do. S and W also assume that there are socially responsible managers who want to do what is right – this might not be a correct assumption and they don't give any examples as evidence of this.

Evaluating

It's a good persuasive argument – seems to be well researched and expert. The article is very clear, well-structured and has detailed points. Their conclusion is supported by evidence, although this is mainly by reference to other authors – I will need to read a couple of these primary sources for myself.

Svensson and Wood argue strongly and clearly that business and society influence each other and, are dependent on each other, and have a responsibility to each other to behave ethically. However, they seem to ignore the fact that not everyone thinks we should trust businesses or that organisations should be responsible to society, and their argument seems to be based on some unproven assumptions. Also, S and W leave out some other simple models of business ethics I've read about and they don't use real business examples for some of their points – they only make references to primary sources that have the examples.

Still, I think that this article is solid enough to use as one of my main sources as evidence for what I think my conclusion will probably be, which is that businesses need to have good ethics and that business ethics is important both to businesses and to society. If anything, reading the article has developed my ideas by making me even more convinced that business ethics is crucial to us all in the wider social context.

Locating

Generally, this article fits in with what I think about the importance of business ethics. The article puts forward a theoretical model which they say has not been done before and that it is therefore doing something new, i.e. filling a gap in theory. They expect other academics to argue or disagree with their model of business ethics.

Svensson and Wood take a similar position to that of Esty, Collins, Shaw and Barry, and on the opposite side to Freidman, Wolf and Carr. I think that this article is an important one on the issue because it is relatively recent and seems to bring together in a detailed and persuasive way, what a lot of the other articles from the last 10 years have said.

Practice 2: how would you question, evaluate and locate this article?

Below are sections from another article (the 1968 article by Albert Carr) the student used for his business ethics essay. Read the sections and then try to question, evaluate and locate the sections. You won't be able to evaluate and locate the article fully, but you should be able to do some critical analysis even without any specific business knowledge.

There is no one correct answer to this exercise, but you can compare your thoughts with those on p. 125.

Is business bluffing ethical?

We can learn a good deal about the nature of business by comparing it with poker. Poker's own brand of ethics is different from the ethical ideals of civilized human relationships as the game calls for distrust of the other fellow . . .

That most businessmen are not indifferent to ethics in their private lives, everyone will agree. My point is that in their office lives they cease to be private citizens; they become game players who must be guided by a somewhat different set of ethical standards . . .

The illusion that business can afford to be guided by ethics as conceived in private life is often fostered by speeches and articles containing such phrases as, 'It pays to be ethical', or, 'Sound ethics is good for business'.

Actually this is not an ethical position at all; it is a self-serving calculation in disguise. The speaker is really saying that in the long run a company can make more money if it does not antagonize competitors, suppliers, employees, and customers by squeezing them too hard. He is saying that overly sharp policies reduce ultimate gains. This is true, but it has nothing to do with ethics.

To be a winner, a man must play to win. This does not mean that he must be ruthless, cruel, harsh, or treacherous. On the contrary, the better his reputation for integrity, honesty, and decency, the better his chances of victory will be in the long run. But from time to time every businessman, like every poker player, is offered a choice between certain loss or bluffing within the legal rules of the game. If he is not resigned to losing, if he wants to rise in his company and industry, then in such a crisis he will bluff- and bluff hard.

Whatever the form of the bluff, it is an integral part of the game, and the executive who does not master its techniques is not likely to accumulate much money or power.

Adapted extracts from: Carr, A. Z. (1968) 'Is business bluffing ethical?' *Harvard Business Review*, 46(1), pp. 143–153.

What should you write down?

Why bother making notes?

The mental and physical process of making notes helps you to understand, think and reflect on what you have read. Making notes also helps you to formulate your own thoughts and ideas, making connections in your mind with other pieces of knowledge. If you don't make notes and just go straight from the text to writing your assignment, you will be bypassing key elements in the critical thinking process, and you will find it harder to develop your own independent understanding of the text. Importantly, making notes also helps you to start using your own words, which is essential for when you come to writing your essay. In summary, making notes helps you to control and exploit your sources rather than letting your sources control your essay.[1]

In addition, making notes (rather than just highlighting or cutting and pasting) will also:

- help you concentrate;
- keep you motivated by tracking and signalling progress;
- help you remember information more easily;
- give you your own unique record of the text;
- save you time when you come to write your assignment.

For all these reasons, students who make notes on their reading usually get better marks than those who go straight from reading a text to writing their essay. However, for your notes to be really effective, they need to be purposeful, clear, meaningful and of real use to you in the essay writing stage. This section gives you some advice, examples and practice to help you write effective notes.

Top tips for making notes

Read first, note later

Try reading the text first without making any notes and then summarise it in your mind or out loud.

Go easy on the highlighter

If you do want to mark the text at a first reading, just pick out the most relevant sections by putting a line down alongside them, using a pencil rather than a highlighter. Remember, though, that you probably won't really get a clear idea of the

---

1 For more advice about making notes, see also Godfrey, J (2009) *Reading and Making Notes*. Palgrave Macmillan.

main points of a text until you have got to the end, and that if you highlight as you read for the first time, you will be stuck with it. A better use of the highlighter might be to use it on your own notes to bring out and emphasise important information.

Do more than just annotate

Annotating a text is fine, but try also to write notes that are separate from the text. Online note-making software usually only allows you to make short annotations on or around the text and so again, also make your own notes either on a separate e-document or on paper.

Explain your reactions to yourself

It's good to react to the text but don't just put **!!** or **?** in the margin – write out your thoughts in full.

Five steps for making notes

Step 1 Have a clear purpose and *make* notes rather than *take* notes

To be effective, your notes need to be purposeful and meaningful. A clear purpose is just as important for note-making as it is for reading – your notes should address the questions you want answered. Think also about the function you want your notes to fulfil. Do you want your notes to:

- extract all the essential points and arguments;
- contain only information on a specific theme;
- focus only on information that addresses your own angle or question;
- clarify the way the points relate to each other and see how the ideas are organised;
- re-organise or connect the text information in a new way?

Remember that you should *make* notes, not *take* notes. Unless you are trying to learn something by heart, there isn't much point in copying down lots of individual sentences or chunks from the text; this usually means that you are on auto-pilot rather than actively reading and thinking. Try to build up the confidence to read and think first and then make notes in your own words that address your own questions. Copy down phrases only if they are really special and powerful.

Step 2 Write down the reference details

You should already have written down the author, title and publication date of each source (called the reference or bibliographic details) when you found them. For books this should include the publishing company and where it was published. These days we are all used to getting information from the media and websites without knowing where it came from. However, in academic study, knowing exactly who wrote something and where the text can be found is vital, as the authors, in a way, own the knowledge or ideas they have communicated in writing (referred to as 'intellectual property').

Write down the bibliographic information fully and accurately, and be careful not to change the case (upper to lower or vice versa) or punctuation of book or article titles.

You should also write down where and how you found the source. This will save you time if you need to go back to check a source, and will help you find new sources in the future.

Below is an example of the student's research record (also called a research log) for the article by Albert Carr. The student found the article by using an e-database on 20 November 2012.

Reference details:
Albert Z. Carr. 1968. 'Is business bluffing ethical?' Harvard Business Review. Vol. 46 Issue 1. pages 143–153.

Comments and search notes:
HBR is a peer-reviewed acad. journal.
Got ref. from list at back of Crane and Matten 2010.
Found it on 20/11/12 in Infolinx – Business Source Complete – Business Resources – Titles – HBR.

Step 3 Make notes on your reading

People make notes in different ways; diagrams, flow charts, bullet points or index cards. You may want to make notes on only parts of the text, on one particular aspect of the text, or on the whole text, depending on why you are reading it. Some people prefer to make notes on paper and others make notes online. Whatever method you use to take notes, you should always:

- note down the reference details, page numbers (particularly for quotations) and the date on which you make your notes;
- read carefully and make accurate notes – don't accidentally change the meaning of the text.

Common student mistakes include:

- not noticing comparatives or superlatives such as *the best / greatest / worst / one of*;
- being inaccurate about the strength, degree or extent of the author's view: for example, if the text says business ethics is *fairly* important, your notes should not report the text as saying that business ethics is *very* important;
- overlooking the words *not* or *no* – if you don't notice these words you may end up with an interpretation that is the opposite of what the text says;
- being imprecise about who says what – if the text paraphrases or quotes *another* author, make sure your notes record this;
- not being precise enough in describing data from graphs, diagrams and tables.

- Make clear in your notes which ideas are major points, which are only examples of these major points, and which are more minor points of information.
- Don't make your notes too brief *or* too detailed.
  If your notes are too brief, the meaning will be unclear and you won't understand them in a month's or year's time. If your notes are too detailed then it probably

means you are copying from the text too much – making notes does not mean copying whole sections from the text.

- Try to use some of your own words and abbreviations.
  You may be worried about changing the meaning of the text accidentally, of 'moving away' from it, or feel that you can't put things into your own words as well as the original. However, you don't have to use *all* your own words, and using some of your own words will help you to start the paraphrasing process. Remember that confidence in using your own words in your notes will increase with practice.
- Have a system that allows you to distinguish between:
  - exact words from the text (quotations);
  - *most* of the same words from the text (close paraphrase);
  - your *own* words to describe ideas in the text (paraphrase);
  - your own ideas or comments.
  You must record these differences carefully so that when you use your notes in your essay you do not accidentally claim source words or ideas as your own. You can use different highlight colours, separate columns, and/or quotation marks for differentiating between quotation, paraphrase and your own comments.

Step 4 Review and rework your notes

Look again at your assignment title and check the focus and relevance of your notes. Familiarise yourself with them and start to put them to work. Ways of doing this include:

- reworking your notes using a different format – linear to pattern or vice versa;
- reorganising your notes around your assignment question title, adding comments and identifying any knowledge gaps;
- reorganising your notes around your own unique question or angle to help develop your own written voice;
- using your notes to write an annotated bibliography.

Step 5 Write a short reflection

Research has shown that students who look back over their notes to check for clarity and meaning and who reflect on them are more successful learners than those who don't. When you have finished making your notes, use them, together with your critical analysis of the text, to write a short reflection. This can be informal and so take any form you find helpful. However, it is a good idea to write in your own words and in full sentences and to use quotation marks for exact phrases from the original text. The reflection should include a short summary of what you have learnt. If the text has a diagram or table, try to summarise what it shows in one sentence.

Writing a short reflection from your notes will consolidate your reading, thinking and questioning, and will maximise the effectiveness of the whole process. It will help you to restate information and ideas from your sources in your own words, and will enable you to further develop your own ideas. Finally, it will help you relate what you have read to what you already know, and will enable you to see how and where you want to use your sources in your essay.

Looking at an example of some notes

Below are the student's notes from the sections of the Svensson and Wood article on pp. 21–22.

	Svensson, G. and Wood, G. (2008) 'A model of business ethics' *Journal of Business Ethics*, 77, pp. 303–322. Notes written on 1/12/2012.
p. 310 true? no model?	In 30 yrs. of BE as a subject, no model of BE – S + W want to fill this gap in BE theory, for debate.
p. 310	'Socially responsible managers do the right thing because it is the right thing to do'.
does it? – don't think so.	Soc. expects the correct action. (CP)
p.319 (conclusion)	Mangs. should want to be ethical because it brings freedom and success. (S + W citing Thomas et al. 2004).
p. 319 main point	BE-'...dynamic and continuous process...' – 'interrelationship between businesses and society . . .' – each responsible for the other.
good point re. importance of BE	BE becoming impt. because people feel that buss. do <u>not</u> behave ethically ∴ the 'mutual obligations need to be restated' (cited from Hoffman and Moore 1982).

Comments on the notes

- The student's notes are brief, but detailed enough to be meaningful. If the first line of the notes had been '*In 30 yrs. no model – S + W want to fill this gap*' this would have been too brief, and when reading these notes at a later stage the student would have been asking himself: '30 years of what?' 'A model of what?' 'What type of gap do they want to fill?'
- Notice how the student has a clear system for recording which parts of the notes are quotation, close paraphrase or paraphrase, and which are his own thoughts. Firstly, he has put phrases and key words taken from the text in quotation marks and has been careful to write down quotes accurately, using three dots to indicate when a quotation is not a whole sentence. Secondly, he has used the letters 'CP' (close paraphrase) to indicate when he has used *mostly* the same words as the text. This is important, as he would need to put such sections much more into his own words if he wanted to use them in his essay (see p. 41). Thirdly, he has used the margin for page numbers and for his own comments and ideas.
- The student has noted when Svensson and Wood have quoted other authors (Thomas et al. and then Hoffman and Moore). This is vital in order to avoid accidentally attributing the ideas of these other authors to Svensson and Wood in his essay.

- You can see that in making notes the student has naturally started the process of using his own words.

Looking at an example of a short reflection

Below is a short reflection on the Svensson and Wood article that the student wrote after reading and critically analysing the text, making notes and then re-reading them. You will notice that by now he is using mostly his own words and style of expression.

> The authors propose and describe their own model of business ethics, which centres around a 'dynamic and continuous process' between business and society. They argue persuasively that business and society influence each other, are dependent on each other and have a responsibility to each other. Importantly, they stress that the ethical standards of society are also those of business and that therefore business ethics is important.
>
> Their model assumes that individuals and society always expect businesses to behave well and that we should be able to trust them. They also assume that good managers exist who are socially responsible. I think that these assumptions may be true some of the time but not all of the time. However, their model is well researched and comprehensive, and is supported by a great deal of other research in the field, and their idea of an 'interrelationship between business and society' accords with the ideas of Esty, Collins and Shaw and Barry. I agree with Svensson and Wood that the way businesses behave does affect society and vice versa, and I will use their article as a key source to support my argument that business ethics is important.

Practice 3: make notes and write a reflection

Before you can come up with a clearer system for making meaningful notes you need to be aware of how you normally *do* take notes. To do this, read and make notes on the extracts from the article by Carr on pp. 22 and 23 (or use a short text of your own if you prefer). Read your notes a week later and compare them with the original text. Check your notes for the following:

- Is the meaning of what you have written clear?
- Can you distinguish between major and minor points?
- Can you distinguish clearly between exact words from the text, mixtures of your own and the author's words, your own words for the author's ideas, and your own ideas?

If anything is unclear, how could you improve the way you make notes so that you really would be able to use them accurately and effectively in an essay?

After you have reviewed and improved your notes, use them together with your critical analysis of the text to write a short reflection. You can compare your notes to the example student notes on p. 126, although, as stated, there is no one correct way of making notes.

Why and how should you quote?

Quotations are phrases or sentences taken from a source unchanged. Below are the last few sentences from the business ethics essay with the quotation the student used given in blue.

> Most importantly, I have shown that businesses are part of society and that they should therefore adhere to the same moral principles, and I have used the 2008 financial collapse as an example of what can happen to society when businesses act unethically. As Trevino and Nelson (2010) state: 'Ethics is not just about the connection we have to other beings – we are all connected; rather, it's about the quality of that connection' (p. 32). I have shown that this is as true in the business context as in any other.

Reasons to quote

Quotations can be a powerful tool when writing an essay but only if you use them sparingly and for the right reasons. Quotations are useful for helping you:

- give a definition;
- state a fact or idea which the author has expressed in a unique and powerful way;
- establish or summarise an author's argument or position;
- provide a powerful and interesting start or end to your essay.

Reasons not to quote

Don't quote someone just because:

- you think that putting quotations in your essay will make it look academic and will impress your tutor;
- some of the articles you have read used lots of quotations so you think your essay should too;
- you have written half of your essay and haven't used any quotations yet, so you think you should put some in;
- you haven't given enough time to reading critically and making notes, so it seems much easier to cut and paste some quotations into your essay rather than putting things into your own words.

How many quotations should you use?

A mistake students often make is to use too many quotations, as most of the time you should restate sources using your own words (for example, only about 4% of the business ethics essay is made up of quotation).

The number of quotations you decide to use will depend on your subject discipline and assignment type, but whatever your topic, you should always ask yourself *why* you are quoting, not how much. You should use quotations only if you think the phrase is particularly interesting or expressed in a powerful and/or unique way.

Indeed, an essay may not have *any* quotations but still be a very successful piece of work because the student has expressed her sources effectively using her own words. Indeed, using too many quotations, for example for more than a quarter of your essay, is a type of plagiarism even if you put in all the correct in-essay references and quotation marks. This is because you can't really claim that your essay is your own work if a significant proportion of it consists of other people's exact words.

Don't overuse quotation marks for individual words

If a specialised term is now a normal part of the language of your discipline, you probably don't need to make it stand out by putting quotation marks around it. If you want to refer to a specialised term coined by a specific author, you can often use italics rather than quotation marks (you can check with your tutor how they want you to mark out special terminology). For example: The term *anomie* refers to a condition of malaise or mild depression.

If you want to refer to a word as a word, you can use quotation marks or italics. For example: People overuse the word 'progress'. *OR* People overuse the word *progress*.

If you want to show that you disagree with how a word has been used, don't just put it in quotation marks and leave it at that; it is often better to put the word in normal font and explain why you disagree with how it has been used. For example: People talk a great deal about 'progress'. ✗

People talk a great deal about progress without really thinking about what it really means. ✔

Looking at examples of quotations used effectively

Below are three slightly adapted extracts from the business ethics essay that contain quotations (given in blue, with their in-essay reference in red). Read the extracts and for each extract, think about why the student decided to use the quotation.

1 Shaw and Barry (2007) **define business ethics as** 'the study of what constitutes right and wrong (or good and bad) human conduct in a business context' (p. 25).

   Another definition describes business ethics as the 'principles and standards that guide behaviour in the world of business' (Ferrell et al. 2002, p. 6).

2 Others, such as Wolf, share the view that businesses do not need to be ethical, and Prindl and Prodham (1994) suggest that 'Finance as practised in the professions and

in industry is seen as a value-neutral positive discipline promoting efficiency without regard to the social consequences which follow from its products' (p. 3).

3 My first proposition is that businesses actually *need* to behave in an ethical manner. This idea is expressed succinctly by Collins (1994) when he states that 'good ethics is synonymous with good management' (p. 2).

Comments on the quotations

The student decided to quote in extract 1 to give examples of different academic definitions of business ethics. In extract 2, the student quoted Prindl and Prodham because he felt that they expressed in a succinct and powerful way the fact that many people in the business world do not feel the need to take an ethical approach. In extract 3 the student uses the quotation to support the main point of his essay, that business ethics is central to business. He also felt that the statement was a very clear and powerful summary by Collins of this idea.

Note that in all three extracts, the student introduces the quotation so that the reader understands why it is being used. In other parts of his essay, the student quotes two individual words, *bluffing* and *dysfunctional* because he felt that these were key words used by the respective authors.

Four steps for using quotations properly

Step 1 Make effective notes

Being able to use quotations effectively is a result of the whole process of selecting and reading with questions in mind, critically evaluating, making meaningful notes, and reflecting on your reading. If you follow this process, you should be able to make good choices in what to quote.

Step 2 Ask yourself why

Before you put a quotation into your essay, ask yourself *why* you are putting it in. Is it special enough? Is it really relevant to your point? Would it not be better to put it into your own words?

Step 3 Give the context and make a comment

When you have written your first draft, separate out each quotation and its surrounding sentences from the rest of your essay. Read each quotation and surrounding sentences slowly and carefully. Make sure you have not taken the quotation out of context and/or misrepresented the author. It is important to show that you understand why the author said what they did before you agree or disagree with them.

Always introduce your quotation clearly and always comment on it, showing clearly how it is relevant to your own point.

Step 4 Be accurate and give an in-essay reference

Once you are sure that your quotation is worth putting in, check that you have quoted accurately, that you have used quotation marks **and** an in-essay reference, and that you have used the correct grammar and punctuation before, during and after the quotation.

Four common mistakes students make with the content of quotations

The four most common and serious mistakes students make with what they quote are:

- using a quotation that is not special enough and where they should, therefore, have used their own words. This includes common facts or knowledge, which don't usually need to be quoted;
- using a quotation that does not directly support their own point;
- not introducing or showing clearly why they have used the quotation;
- using a reporting verb (e.g. *states, shows, suggests, points out, claims*) that is not correct for the context and function of the quotation (see section B1).

Practice 4: would you use these quotations?

Below are some quotations from several student essays on bioscience topics. Read them and identify which of the above mistakes the students have made. Answers are on p. 127.

1 Kzanty (2004) states that 'Organs such as the heart, liver, small bowel, pancreas and lungs are used for transplants' (p.11).
2 Logan (1999) states that 'The second world war ended in 1945' (p.111).
3 The main benefit of organ transplant is that it saves lives. As stated by Smith (2005), 'heart transplantation can save lives, but the procedure carries serious risks and complications and a high mortality rate' (p. 12).
4 Improvements in transplantation have made it possible for animal organs to be used. This is beneficial, as patients are not forced to wait for transplants. As stated by Kline (2005): 'advances in genetic techniques mean that there is less chance of animal organs being rejected by the human immune system' (p. 53).
5 Transplantation carries the risk of being attacked by the immune system and the patient is therefore at risk or organ failure again. As stated by Smith (2005): 'Everyone reported common side effects which included diarrhoea, edemas, fatigue and ulcers' (p. 5).

Three common mistakes students make with in-essay references for quotations

The three most common serious mistakes students make when referencing quotations are:

- **Not using both quotation marks *and* an in-essay reference**
  Some students make the mistake of using quotation marks but not an in-essay reference because they think that using quotation marks and a reference in the bibliography at the end of the essay are enough. Other students make the mistake of giving an in-essay reference but not using quotation marks because they think that the in-essay reference is enough. In academic writing, however, giving an in-essay reference and no quotation marks always indicates that you are expressing an idea from a source *in your own words*. Therefore, quoting without using quotation

marks is plagiarism (claiming someone else's words or ideas as your own) even if you have given an in-essay reference. The only time you do not use quotation marks is for longer quotations (more than three sentences) in which case indentation is used instead of quotation marks.

Look again at essay extracts 1–3 on p. 31 and notice how the student uses both quotation marks *and* an in-essay reference with each quotation.

- **Giving only an in-essay reference for a primary source that was read in a secondary text**
  You must make clear in your essay which book or article you have actually read. In the essay extract below (one that was not used in the final essay) the student correctly uses the phrase *cited in* to show that he did not actually read the Hoffman and Moore article, but read a quotation from their work in the article by Svensson and Wood. It would be poor scholarship, and a misrepresentation of what you have read, to give only the reference for Hoffman and Moore.

  > Hoffman and Moore (1982) suggest that the public feels that businesses fail to behave in a socially acceptable manner and that 'the mutual obligations of business to the community and the community to business need to be restated' (Hoffman and Moore 1982, cited in Svensson and Wood 2008).

- **Putting parentheses (round brackets) in the wrong place**
  Look again at the extract from the business ethics essay below. Notice that for the first quotation, because the student uses Shaw and Barry as part of the introductory sentence, he uses parentheses only for the year of publication and for the page number. For the second quotation however, the student does not use the authors Ferrell et al. as part of his sentence, so both the names and year of publication date are in parentheses at the end of the quotation.

  > Shaw and Barry (2007) define it as 'the study of what constitutes right and wrong (or good and bad) human conduct in a business context' (p. 25). Another definition describes business ethics as the 'principles and standards that guide behaviour in the world of business' (Ferrell et al. 2002, p. 6).

Practice 5: are these quotations referenced properly?

Below are four incorrect versions of the first part of essay extract 1 on p. 31. Look at these altered versions and identify what the mistakes are in how the quotations have been referenced.

1 Business ethics is the study of what constitutes right and wrong (or good and bad) human conduct in a business context.
2 Shaw and Barry (2007) define business ethics as the study of what constitutes right and wrong (or good and bad) human conduct in a business context (p. 25).
3 Business ethics is 'the study of what constitutes right and wrong (or good and bad) human conduct in a business context'.
4 (Shaw and Barry 2007) define business ethics as 'the study of what constitutes right and wrong (or good and bad) human conduct in a business context'.

Four common mistakes students make with structure, grammar or punctuation when using quotations

It's important not to accidentally misrepresent an author because of the way you structure or integrate a quotation into your writing. The most common mistakes students make with this are:

- **Changing words or other elements in the quotation**
  You must not change any words or spellings or do anything that leads to a misrepresentation of the quotation. If there is a mistake or non-standard usage in the quotation, you can choose to add *sic* in square brackets immediately after the item to inform your reader that it is not your mistake. *Sic* is the abbreviated form of the Latin phrase *sic erat scriptum* meaning 'thus was it written'. For example: 'The guidelines state that 'staff should discuss all problems with there [sic] manager'.

- If you need to add a word of your own to make the quotation fit with your surrounding sentence or to clarify its meaning, use a square bracket to show that you have added something that was not in the original text. For example: Emille (2002) states that 'they [the public] only hear what they want to hear' (p. 10). The one change you are allowed to make without using square brackets is to change the first letter of a quotation from upper to lower case, so that your quotation integrates smoothly into the rest of your sentence. If you want to leave out part of a quotation, use an ellipsis (three dots with a space in between each one) to indicate that you have done so. As an example, below is an extract from the article by Albert Carr followed by a quotation used in a student essay. In the quotation, the student has used an ellipsis and has also changed the first letter of the quotation from 'T' to 't' so that it fits in with her sentence. Extract:

  > The illusion that business can afford to be guided by ethics as conceived in private life is often fostered by speeches and articles containing such phrases as, 'It pays to be ethical,' or, 'Sound ethics is good for business'. Actually this is not an ethical position at all; it is a self-serving calculation in disguise.

  Quotation from the extract:

  > Carr (1968) states that 'the illusion that business can afford to be guided by ethics . . . is a self-serving calculation in disguise'.

  You do not usually need to use an ellipsis to show that you have missed out the *start* of the sentence in a quotation, as long as this does not lead to a misrepresentation of what the author is saying; if it does then do use ellipsis to start the quotation. Note that the use of the ellipsis varies slightly between different referencing styles, so check your referencing guide.

- **Putting in an extra *he / she / it /they* or topic word before a quotation**
  If you use the author's name as the subject of your introductory sentence, you should not use also a subject pronoun such as he or it. Equally, if you use the topic word (e.g. 'business ethics') in your introductory sentence, you should not repeat it in the quotation.

- **Using the wrong punctuation in front of a quotation**
  Use a colon if you use a complete phrase (called an independent clause) to

introduce a quotation. For instance: Carr's central maxim is very clear: 'To be a winner a man must play to win' (p. 153).

Carr makes the following statement: 'To be a winner a man must play to win' (p. 153).

Use a comma if you use an introductory, incomplete phrase to introduce a quotation. For instance: As Tomalin (2010) states, 'Pepys was . . . mapping a recognizably modern world' (p. 148).

According to Brandon (2008), 'History is a record of relationships' (p. 151).

Don't use any punctuation if you integrate your quotation smoothly into the rest of your sentence. For instance:

> This idea is expressed succinctly by Collins (1994) when he states that 'good ethics is synonymous with good management' (p. 2).

- **Putting punctuation marks in the wrong place at the end of a quotation**
  Don't worry too much about making small mistakes with the punctuation of quotations but do try to develop correct use over time. Keep question marks and other punctuation from the original text inside the quotation marks. The exception to this is the full-stop; for the author/date in-essay reference style you should put the full-stop at the very end, after the page number brackets.

Practice 6: is the grammar and punctuation of these quotations correct?

Below is one of the extracts from the business ethics essay followed by four incorrect versions. Identify the mistakes in each incorrect version.

Correct essay extract*

> My first proposition is that businesses actually *need* to behave in an ethical manner. This idea is expressed succinctly by Collins (1994) when he states that 'good ethics is synonymous with good management' (p. 2).

Incorrect versions

1 My first proposition is that businesses actually *need* to behave in an ethical manner. This idea is expressed succinctly by Collins (1994) when he states that 'good business ethics is synonymous with good management' (p. 2).

2 My first proposition is that businesses actually *need* to behave in an ethical manner. This idea is expressed succinctly by Collins (1994) when he states that 'good ethics is good management' (p. 2).

3 My first proposition is that businesses actually *need* to behave in an ethical manner. This idea is expressed succinctly by Collins (1994) when talking about good ethics that 'good ethics is synonymous with good management' (p. 2).

4 My first proposition is that businesses actually *need* to behave in an ethical manner. This idea is expressed succinctly by Collins (1994) when he states that 'good ethics is synonymous with good management.' (p. 2)

*The answer section on pp. 127–128 includes a correct version of this extract using the numeric referencing system.

Why and how should you paraphrase?

Paraphrasing is when you express one specific idea or piece of information from a short section of source text, using your own words and style. Being able to paraphrase well is central to academic writing, and is also an ability employers look for in graduates. This section gives you essential points on paraphrasing, takes you through some examples of good and poor paraphrasing, and gives you a short practice exercise to help you acquire this complex skill.

Why paraphrase?

Restating what you have read in your own way allows you to:

- go through a mental process that helps you to understand and think about what you have read in a more independent way;
- express the information and ideas from sources in your own style of thinking and writing so that you can integrate them smoothly into your argument and essay;
- restate information and ideas from sources in a way that best supports your own argument;
- show your tutor that you have understood what you have read and how you have used it to develop your knowledge and ideas;
- express information and ideas from complicated texts more clearly and simply;
- restate information and ideas from your sources that are not special enough to quote.

Looking at examples of good paraphrasing

Below are two extracts from a book the student read for his business ethics essay. Each extract is followed by the section in his essay where he introduces his own point and then paraphrases from the source (in blue). Read and compare the source extracts with the paraphrases in the essay extracts.

Source extract 1

> . . . amazon.com currently stocks more than 14,000 books related to business ethics and corporate responsibility, whilst a Google search on 'business ethics' returns more than 4 million hits at the time of writing. . . . One annual UK survey, for instance, estimates the country's 'ethical market' (i.e. consumer spending on ethical products and services) to be worth something like £35bn annually (The Co-operative Bank 2008).
>
> Extract from: Crane, A. and Matten D. (2010) *Business Ethics*. p. 14.

Essay extract 1

Over the past couple of decades, the ethical credentials of businesses appear to have become an explicit factor in consumer choice. . . . The UK ethical market is valued at over 30 billion euros per year, and there are currently over 14,000 books and 4 million web entries related to business ethics (The Co-operative Bank 2008, cited in Crane and Matten, 2010).

Source extract 2

. . . there is indeed considerable overlap between ethics and the law. In fact, the law is essentially and institutionalisation or codification of ethics into specific social rules, regulations, and proscriptions. Nevertheless, the two are not equivalent. . . . The law might be said to be a definition of the minimum acceptable standards of behaviour. However, many morally contestable issues, whether in business of elsewhere, are not explicitly covered by the law. . . . In one sense then, business ethics can be said to begin where the law ends. Business ethics is primarily concerned with those issues not covered by the law, or where there is no definite consensus on whether something is right or wrong.

Extracts from: Crane, A. and Matten, D. (2010) *Business Ethics*. pp. 5 and 7.

Essay extract 2

It is important to emphasise here that business ethics is not synonymous with legality. There is some overlap between law and ethics, but legislation usually only regulates the lowest level of acceptable behaviour (Crane and Matten 2010). In addition, as Trevino and Nelson (2010) point out, the law is limited in what it can do to prevent unacceptable actions, because legislation follows rather than precedes trends in behaviour. Business ethics then, as Crane and Matten state, is mainly concerned with areas of conduct that are *not* specifically covered by law and that are therefore open to different interpretations, a fact that means a particular behaviour may be legal albeit viewed as unethical.

Comments on the paraphrases

Notice how the student has not just replaced individual words in his paraphrases. His paraphrases are a complete rewriting of the source, based on his independent understanding of the texts, and written from his notes in his own style so that they make sense to him. His paraphrases are less complex than the original and he has changed the order of the information.

In essay extract 2 the student has emphasised the fact that ethics is not the same thing as the law. He has emphasised this difference because in this part of his essay he is defining and describing what business ethics is, and so wants to point out the differences between business ethics, the law and morality.

Notice that both paraphrases are shorter than the original. A paraphrase can be as long and as detailed as the original text but will often be shorter because the points are condensed and/or the language and sentence structure is simpler. Paraphrase 1 is shorter than the original extract because the student has used this paraphrase in his essay introduction as just a brief example of the importance of business ethics.

Paraphrase 2 is also shorter than the original extract because although the student has included all the points from the original source, he has used simpler language and condensed the ideas in his own way.

Five key points for paraphrasing

1   Check that your paraphrase clearly supports the point *you* are making
Don't let your paraphrases take control of your essay. Decide what point you want to make and then check that your paraphrase is relevant. Make sure that you comment on the paraphrase, showing how it supports your point. Check that you have reported the source information accurately and that you have used reporting verbs (e.g. *show, suggest, claim*) in such a way as to give the emphasis which best supports your argument (see section B1).

2   Write your paraphrase from your notes and reflection, not straight from the original text
If you have approached your reading in a similar way to that suggested in sections A1, A2 and A3, you will already be well on the way to writing good paraphrases. Using your own words will be much easier if you have gone through the process of making good notes and writing a reflection on your reading. Remember that your paraphrase should be your own understanding and rewriting of short sections of a source, not a translation straight from the text.

3   Use your own words and writing style
When you paraphrase you must use your own words as far as possible – around 90% of the wording should be your own. The rules of academic writing do not allow you to change only a few words or even half of the words from the original text, as this would be plagiarism. You must either change nothing and use the source as a quotation, or rewrite the source as a paraphrase, using about 90% of your own words. The pattern and structure of your sentences should also be your own as far as possible.

Keeping words from the original text
There will be some words or short phrases you can't change; in the example paraphrases these words are *business ethics, ethical market, law* and *behaviour*. You do not need to put quotation marks around such commonly used words. However, if you are keeping a word from the source that the author has used in a unique or special way, or if the word is a new term coined by the author, you should use it as a one-word quotation and put quotation marks around it. Always check that you have not accidentally used the same words or sentence patterns as the original text unless absolutely necessary.

You should also try to rephrase statistics. For example, *one fifth* can also be expressed as *20%*, and *more than double* can be expressed as *over twice as many / much*. It may not always be possible or make sense to rephrase numbers and statistics but you should do this if you can.

4   Always use an in-essay reference
Using in-essay references with your paraphrases is essential, not optional. In academic writing, if something is not referenced, it is assumed to be both your own words *and* your own idea. You

must therefore *always* give in-essay references when paraphrasing, because the ideas and information you have restated are not yours, even though you have used your own words. Not giving an in-essay reference for paraphrases is the most common cause of of accidental student plagiarism.

Giving in-essay references is also an important way of getting marks. Your in-essay references will show your tutor that you have done some reading and that you have understood it. In-essay references also show your tutor (and yourself) how your reading has helped you to develop your own ideas.

5   Use reference reminder phrases

Giving an in-essay reference at the start of your paraphrase will often not be enough. In essay extracts 1 and 2 above, the student gives an in-essay reference at the end of the first sentence of each paraphrase. This is enough for these paraphrases because they are only one sentence long. If a paraphrase is more than one sentence long, however, you will probably need to use what I call a 'reference reminder phrase'.

Below is an example of another section from the business ethics essay in which the student paraphrases from Carr. The student has used the reference reminder phrase *he suggests that* to make clear that the ideas in the second sentence are also those of Carr. If this phrase were deleted from the essay extract, the tutor might assume that the idea in the second sentence was that of the student.

Carr (1968) uses the analogy of a poker game to argue that a successful businessman needs to play by the rules of the industry and that these include 'bluffing' as an acceptable form of behaviour. He suggests that what is, in effect, lying is merely part of legitimate business strategy, and that business rules do not need to take account of personal or social principles.

If you don't use reference reminder phrases, it may become unclear in your essay which of your sentences express your own ideas and which ones express the ideas of other authors. This lack of clarity could lead you to plagiarise accidentally because as stated above, it is always assumed in academic writing that anything that is not referenced is your own comment or idea.

How much of your essay should consist of paraphrases?

This will depend on how many sources you use, your subject and on your assignment title and type. If you are conducting your own experiment or research, you may not be using many sources and therefore not paraphrasing. However, most types of undergraduate essay will consist of many short paraphrases from different sources. If you look at some academic journal articles in your subject you will see that some of them have about 50% of their content in the form of paraphrase (from lots of different sources and therefore with lots of different in-essay references). The business ethics essay has about 50% of its word count as paraphrase, but is still original because of the student's choice of sources and how he has used and evaluated them. However, try not to end up with lots of short paraphrases that are merely strung together by individual phrases or sentences of your own. If you find yourself doing this, go back and do some more thinking about what your argument is. Then try to emphasise your own argument more in your writing, summarise your sources more, and give more of your own evaluations and comments on sources to show how they support your points.

Four common mistakes students make when paraphrasing

- **Not showing clearly where a paraphrase begins and ends**
  Student essays often do not show clearly enough which sentences are their own words and ideas and which sentences are paraphrases of sources. For example, if you only give one in-essay reference in brackets at the end of a long paragraph, it probably won't be clear which sentences in that paragraph are paraphrase and which sentences are your own points. As discussed in the key points above, you must use both in-essay references and reference reminder phrases.

- **Not making enough changes from the original source**
  Students sometimes use just a few of their own words to sew together unchanged sentences or phrases from a source or from several different sources. Even if you give the relevant in-essay references, this type of 'sewing' is plagiarism because most of the words and style are not your own.

- **Changing individual words but keeping the same sentence pattern as the original**
  This might happen if you don't make notes and reflect on your reading but just try to 'translate' word by word from the text straight into your essay. Even if you change all the words, your paraphrase will still have the same style and pattern of the original text and this is therefore still a type of plagiarism.

- **Accidentally changing the meaning of the original text**
  This might happen if you have not read and understood the text carefully enough, not thought critically about it or have not made clear notes. Make sure you understand from the text what is fact and what is opinion and pay particular attention to small but important words such as *no*, *not* or *not as* and comparatives such as *faster*. For example, saying that smoking cannabis is *not as* damaging as smoking cigarettes is very different from saying that smoking cannabis is not damaging.

Looking at some examples of poor paraphrasing

Below is a short extract from a journal article that looks at whether mobile phones are a health risk.

The extract is followed by three unacceptable paraphrases which all try to use this article to support the view that mobile phones do not damage health. Read the extract and then the unacceptable paraphrases. Finally, read the comments and the example of a good paraphrase of the article extract.

Source extract

So far there is no clear evidence from health studies of a relation between mobile phone use and mortality or morbidity. Indeed, tantalising findings in humans include a speeding up of reaction time during exposure, particularly during behavioural tasks calling for attention and electrical brain activity changes during cognitive processes. It is not clear, however, whether these findings have any positive implications for health.

Adapted from: Maier, M., Blakemore, C. and Koivisto, M. (2000)
'The health hazards of mobile phones' *British Medical Journal*,
320(7245), pp. 1288–1289.

Unacceptable paraphrases

1 Maier et al. (2000) show that there is no clear evidence from health studies of a relation between mobile phone use and mortality or morbidity. They state that in fact, tantalising findings in humans include a speeding up of reaction time during exposure, particularly during behavioural tasks calling for attention and changes in brain electricity during cognitive processes. It is not clear, however, whether these findings have any positive implications for health.

2 Some studies point to interesting results which suggest that while using a phone, the user has quicker reaction times to some behavioural tasks (Maier et al. 2000). In fact, there are interesting findings in humans that show a speeding up of reaction time during exposure, particularly during behavioural tasks calling for attention and changes in brain electricity during cognitive processes. It is unclear whether these findings have any positive implications for health.

3 Maier et al. (2000) show that up to now there is not any strong proof from studies on disease, of a link between the use of mobile phones and death or disease. In fact, interesting results in humans include a faster time of reaction during use, especially while doing practical tasks that need concentration and brain electricity change during the thought process. It is unclear whether these results imply any health benefits (ibid.)

et al. = and the other authors.
ibid. = from the same source as previously mentioned.

Comments on the unacceptable paraphrases

Paraphrase 1

The student has correctly used an in-essay reference and the reference reminder phrase *They state that*. However, the only changes she has made from the source it to put in these references, take off the first two words and reword the phrase 'electrical brain activity changes'. Everything else is copied word for word from the source without any use of quotation marks. This is plagiarism.

Paraphrase 2

The student has used an in-essay reference and has also made some significant changes in wording. However, there are two problems with this paraphrase. The first is that there are still several long phrases which are unchanged from the original source (underlined below). This could be seen as plagiarism. Secondly, there is no reference reminder phrase and so the reader is not sure whether the information in the second sentence comes from Maier et al. or from the student. By the time the reader gets to the third sentence, it could easily be assumed that the point expressed in this sentence is that of the student and this could therefore be seen as plagiarism. To summarise, this paraphrase contains plagiarism on two counts; lack of adequate referencing and phrases copied from the original source.

Paraphrase 2 with phrases from the source underlined:

Some studies point to interesting results which suggest that while using a phone, the user has quicker reaction times to some behavioural tasks (Maier et al. 2000). In fact, there are interesting <u>findings in humans</u> that show <u>a speeding up of reaction time during exposure, particularly during behavioural tasks calling for attention</u> and changes in brain electricity <u>during cognitive processes</u>. It is unclear <u>whether these findings have any positive implications for health</u>.

Paraphrase 3

The student has used nearly all her own words and has used two in-essay references. However, she has merely translated the original word by word as she goes along. The student has been too dependent on her source and instead of making and using notes, has gone straight from reading the article to writing her paraphrase. The result is a paraphrase that has exactly the same 'pattern' as the original. This does not show a clear understanding of the original or control of her source and is a type of plagiarism.

An example of a good paraphrase of the extract

Studies point to interesting results suggesting that mobile phone users experience quicker reaction times to tasks which require both changes in electrical brain activity and concentration (Maier et al. 2000). Although it has not been shown that that this effect represents an actual benefit to health, there has equally been no data from any disease studies to suggest that mobile phones actually damage health in any way (ibid.).

Practice 7: what do you think of these paraphrases?

Below is a short extract from a different article on the issue of mobile phones and health risks. Underneath the extracts are four unacceptable paraphrases. Read the extract and then the paraphrases and identify what is wrong with each one. Two examples of good paraphrases are given on p. 128, one using author/date referencing and the other numeric referencing.

Source extract

Mobile phones provide an interesting example of a source risk to health which may be largely non-existent but which cannot be totally dismissed. Such risks, when possibly serious and with long-term consequences, are typically dealt with by appeal to the so-called precautionary principle but, of course, precaution comes at a price.

Cox, D.R. (2003) 'Communication of risk: health hazards from mobile phones'
Journal of the Royal Statistical Society: Series A (Statistics in Society),
166(2), pp. 214–246.

Unacceptable paraphrases

1 Advising caution in the use of mobile phones is an example of a typical approach to the fear of a possible health risk which may be of a serious nature. Such an approach may have negative consequences, but is taken because although there may in fact be no health risk, this has not yet been proven.

2 Cox (2003) suggests that advising caution in the use of mobile phones is an example of a typical approach to the fear of a possible health risk which may be of a serious nature. Such an approach may have negative consequences, but is taken because although there may in fact be no health risk, this has not yet been proven.

3 Advising caution in the use of mobile phones is an example of a typical approach to the fear of a possible health risk which may be of a serious nature. Such an approach may have negative consequences but is taken because although there may in fact be no health risk, this has not yet been proven (Cox 2003).

4 Mobile phones provide an interesting example of a source risk to health which may be largely non-existent but which cannot be totally dismissed (Cox 2003). So far there is no clear evidence from health studies of a relation between mobile phone use and mortality or morbidity.

Practice 8: write your own paraphrase

Paraphrase the source extract below. An example of an acceptable paraphrase is given on p. 129.

Source extract

The National Radiological Protection Board said that more than 50 million mobile phones are used in the UK today, a number that has doubled since 2000. The mobile phone industry has contended that no research has shown that mobile phone use is hazardous to the health of the public.

Adapted from: Telecommunications Reports (2005) 'U.K. finds "No hard evidence" of cellphone health risk' 71(2), pp. 19–20.

Why and how should you summarise?

Summarising a source is when you express its main points in your own way, using your own words. Both paraphrasing and summarising sources require you to use your own words and in-essay references, but while a paraphrase expresses *all* the information contained in a specific part of a text, a summary gives only the *main* points from a much larger section or from the whole text. Summarising is a complex skill and one that is central to academic writing and that you will need both at university and in your future career. This section gives you key points and steps for summarising, looks at common problems, and gives examples of good and poor summarising.

Why summarise?

Summarising is a key element in writing essays and other types of assignment, and is important for the same reasons for paraphrasing (see p. 37). However, a summary can be an even more powerful writing tool than a paraphrase because it allows you to show that you have understood the key point of a text and that you can express this clearly in your own way. Summarising therefore allows you great control over your use of sources.

There are two main reasons for giving a summary of a source in your essay:

- to give evidence and support for your own argument;
- to give an overview of different authors who support a particular position.
  An overview is commonly given near the beginning of an essay, although you can give a brief overview of the literature at any stage in your essay when you are setting the scene for a specific point in your argument. Giving a summary of the position of key authors (see p. 46) shows that you understand where they locate themselves in the subject.

How long should a summary be?

The length and level of detail of your summary will depend on what you want it to do in your essay. A summary that includes all the main points of a text may be up to a third as long as the original text. Often however, you will want to give a very brief summary of only a few sentences or even just one phrase that expresses the key point of the text.

Looking at some examples of summaries

Below are two separate extracts you will recognise from the business ethics essay. Read each extract and think about why and how the student has briefly summarised his sources in the essay (the summaries are in blue) and then read the comments on each extract.

Essay extract 1

Opponents of the concept of ethics in business include those who claim that making a profit is the only responsibility a business has to society (Friedman 1970, cited in Fisher and Lovell 2003). Others such as Wolf (2008) share this view, and Prindl and Prodham (1994) suggest that 'Finance as practised in the professions and in industry is seen as a value-neutral positive discipline, promoting efficiency without regard to the social consequences which follow from its products' (p. 3). Carr (1968) uses the analogy of a poker game to argue that a successful businessman needs to play by the rules of the industry and that these include 'bluffing' as an acceptable form of behaviour. He suggests that what is, in effect, lying is merely part of legitimate business strategy and that business rules do not need to take account of personal or social principles.

Essay extract 2

My first proposition is that businesses actually *need* to behave in an ethical manner. This idea is expressed succinctly by Collins (1994) when he states that 'good ethics is synonymous with good management' (p. 2). Collins states that if managers only concern themselves with profit, they will become 'dysfunctional'. This is because any business is made up of people: employees, customers and other stakeholders. He states that if businesses do not operate with a degree of trust, co-operation and consideration both inside the organisation and externally, they will in fact be putting constraints on profitability. This idea of the interdependence of any business organisation is also supported by Shaw and Barry (2007), Green (1994), Fritzsche (2005) and Svensson and Wood (2008).

Comments on the extracts

In essay extract 1, the student summarises the view of Friedman in one sentence and then summarises the position of Wolf in only three words by stating that Wolf shares the same view. The student then uses a key quotation as a type of summary to state the position of Prindl and Prodham. The extract ends with a one-sentence summary of Carr's position. The extract gives an effective overview of key authors who oppose the idea that business ethics are important.

In essay extract 2, the student first establishes his own point by using a key quotation which also acts as a summary of Collins' position. He then explains Collins' view in a bit more detail by giving a two-sentence summary. In the final sentence of the extract the student summarises the main point of four other articles and six authors in a phrase of only 13 words: 'This idea of the interdependence of any business organisation is also supported by...' By doing all of this, the student shows that he understands the key point of all of these texts and also emphasises that these authors all hold a similar position on the issue.

Five points to remember when summarising

- Express only the main point or points in the text.
- Give an objective and balanced summary of these points and do not include your own opinion or comments.
- As with paraphrasing, your summary should be your own expression, style and words as far as possible. It is not acceptable to change only a few words of the original text or to sew together key sentences copied from the text.
- As with paraphrasing, you must always give in-essay references with your summary, because the ideas and information you have restated are not yours, even though the way you have expressed them is. Summarising without giving an in-essay reference is a form of plagiarism.
- As with paraphrasing, if your summary is more than one sentence long, check whether you need to use reference reminder phrases to make clear that the later sentences are still points from your source.

Five steps for writing good summaries

Step 1 Identify how the source text is organised

Writing a good summary starts with your reading. Make sure that you understand how the text is structured. Read the title, sub-headings, introduction and conclusion of the text to help you identify the key points. Identify which parts of the text are main points and which are examples of these points or more minor points.

Step 2 Understand, make clear notes and critically reflect on your reading

If you have approached your reading in a similar way to the steps given in section A1, A2 and A3, you will already be well on the way to writing a good summary. If you have written a critical reflection on what you have read it probably already includes a summary of the text.

Step 3 Summarise what the text is about in one or two sentences

A really useful exercise is to use your notes to write a very short summary of only one or two sentences. Doing this helps you to clarify in your mind what the main point of the text is. If you need to, you can then write a longer, more detailed summary that includes all the main points.

Step 4 Think about why and how you want to use the summary

Before you put your summary into your essay, ask yourself how it fits into your essay plan and argument. Make sure you show clearly how your summary supports your own point.

Step 5 Check that you have used your own words and style, in-essay references, and reference reminder phrases

As with paraphrasing, check that you have written your summary using your own words as far as possible and that you have used adequate in-essay referencing.

Six common mistakes students make when summarising:

- accidently changing the meaning of the original text;
- giving too much detail and putting in minor points, examples or definitions from the text, rather than just the main points;
- adding their own opinion or comments;
- not making enough changes in words and style from the original source;
- not making clear where the summary begins and ends (i.e. not using clear in-essay references and reference reminder phrases);
- giving the primary source as the in-essay reference when they have only read the secondary source.

Practice 9: what's wrong with these summaries?

Below is a short text. Read it and make your own notes. Use your notes to write first a one-sentence summary of the text, then a summary of three or four sentences. After you have written your own summaries, read the five unacceptable summaries and identify what is wrong with them. Finally, read the comments on the unacceptable summaries and then look at the good summaries.

A study on links between emotion regulation, job satisfaction and intentions to quit

Emotion regulation is the conscious and unconscious efforts people make to increase, maintain or decrease their emotions and is manifested by changes in facial expression and by changes in vocal and body signals. People often regulate their emotions at work. An example of emotion suppression is when a worker tries to hide anger they might be feeling towards a colleague or manager. Emotion amplification on the other hand, is when one pretends to be happier than one actually is. For example, an insurance or telephone salesperson may amplify their display of positive emotion to customers in order to increase their level of sales and quality of service.

Cote and Morgan (2002) conducted a study that looks at the relationship between emotion regulation, job satisfaction and intention to quit one's job. They collected two sets of data from 111 workers. The participants gave informed consent and were asked to complete two questionnaires on how they felt they had regulated their emotions at work and their feelings about their job. There was a time interval of four weeks between the two questionnaires to allow enough time for changes in emotion regulation but also to have a short enough period to maintain the retention of the participants.

Cote and Morgan showed from their data that the amplification of pleasant emotions happened more frequently than the suppression of unpleasant emotions. Importantly, they also found a strong correlation between emotion regulation and job satisfaction and intention to quit. They demonstrated that, as they predicted, the suppression of unpleasant emotions leads to a decrease in job satisfaction and therefore an increase in intention to quit. Their findings also suggest that an increase in the amplification of pleasant emotions will increase job satisfaction, because it increases positive social interaction and more positive responses from colleagues and customers.

Although their experiment showed that emotion regulation affects job satisfaction, there was no strong evidence to suggest a reverse correlation i.e. that job satisfaction and intention to quit influence emotional regulation.

Source: Robinson, J. (2011) 'A study on links between emotion regulation, job satisfaction and intentions to quit' *Business Reports that Matter* (3) p. 41.

Unacceptable summaries

1 Emotion regulation is the conscious and unconscious efforts people make to increase, maintain or decrease their emotions. Cote and Morgan (2002) have conducted a study that looks at the relationship between emotion regulation, job satisfaction and intention to quit one's job. Cote and Morgan showed from their data that the amplification of pleasant emotions happened more frequently than the suppression of unpleasant emotions. Importantly, they also found a strong correlation between emotion regulation and job satisfaction and intention to quit.

2 A study has shown a strong link between emotion regulation and job satisfaction and intention to quit (Cote and Morgan 2002, cited in Robinson, 2011). An example of emotion regulation is when someone attempts to hide the anger they feel towards their boss or when they pretend to be happier than they really are during a work meeting or when dealing with customers. Cote and Morgan tested 111 workers by asking them to complete two questionnaires at an interval of four weeks. They found and that workers exaggerate positive emotions more than they hide negative feelings. The findings also showed that suppressing negative feelings leads to lower job satisfaction and that amplifying positive feelings leads to better work relationships and therefore higher job satisfaction.

3 Robinson (2011) describes a study conducted by Cote and Morgan, in which they obtained data on emotion regulation from 111 workers. The findings suggest that workers exaggerate positive emotions more than they hide negative feelings and that there is strong evidence that how you feel about your job influences how you regulate your emotions at work.

4 A study has shown a strong link between emotion regulation and job satisfaction and intention to quit (Cote and Morgan 2002, cited in Robinson, 2011) and that workers exaggerate positive emotions more than they hide negative feelings. This might be because workers are worried that if they show their negative feelings, they might not get promoted, or worse, that they may lose their job. The findings also showed that suppressing negative feelings leads to a decrease in job satisfaction and a corresponding increase in wanting to leave, and that amplifying positive feelings leads to more positive interaction at work and therefore more job satisfaction.

Comments on the unacceptable summaries

Summary 1 consists of four key sentences copied word for word from the original text. This is therefore plagiarism. In addition to this, the student has only given an in-essay reference for Cote and Morgan, which implies that they have read the primary Cote and Morgan article, when in fact they have only read the Robinson text. This is a misrepresentation of both Cote and Morgan and of what the student has read.

The first and the last two sentences of summary 2 are good, with correct in-essay references. However, in the middle of the summary the student has included different examples of what emotion regulation is and also details of the method of the study, neither of which should be in a summary.

Summary 3 starts with a correct in-essay reference, and the summary is written in the student's own words and style, which is good. However, the last point in the summary is not correct – the study showed that emotion regulation can influence how you feel about your job but that there was *no* evidence that job satisfaction affects emotion regulation.

Summary 4 starts and ends well, with a clear statement of the key point and correct in-essay references. However, the second sentence is the student's own idea of why workers might hide negative feelings, and this should not be part of the summary. Any comments or opinion by the student on the results of the Cote and Morgan study should come after the summary rather than within it.

An example of an acceptable one-sentence summary

A study has shown a strong link between regulating emotions at work and job satisfaction levels, and therefore intention to quit (Cote and Morgan 2002, cited in Robinson 2011).

An example of an acceptable three-sentence summary

A study has shown that people exaggerate positive emotions more than they hide negative feelings when at work (Cote and Morgan 2002, cited in Robinson 2011). Cote and Morgan established a strong link between regulating emotions, job satisfaction and intention to quit. They found that suppressing negative feelings leads to lower levels of job satisfaction, and that amplifying positive feelings leads to better relationships at work and therefore more job satisfaction. However, they found no evidence of job satisfaction level affecting how people regulate their emotions at work.

Practice 10: write a summary

Read and make notes on the informative source text below. From your notes, write a one-sentence summary and then a two- or three-sentence summary. Each summary should include an in-essay reference and reference reminder phrase. Compare your summaries with the examples given on p. 129.

Source text

Sport in the UK: the role of the DCMS
The Department for Culture, Media and Sport (DCMS) is responsible for delivering Government policy on sport, from supporting the performance and preparation of elite individual performers and teams to increasing sporting opportunities at all levels, but especially for the young, to encourage long-lasting participation.

DCMS recognizes that success in sport by UK representatives at the elite level, such as athletes at the Olympics or football teams in European competition, can enhance the reputation of the country and make large numbers of people feel proud. To that end, it provides funding where it will make a difference, such as through the Talented Athlete Scholarship Scheme, and political support where that is more suitable, such as to the Football Association's attempts to be awarded the right to host the 2018 FIFA World Cup in England.

DCMS also supports opportunities to participate in sport in schools and communities, regardless of the level of performance. Among DCMS' targets are that by 2008, 85% of 5–16-year-olds will be taking physical education and other school sports for a minimum of two hours per week, and that by 2012 all children will have the opportunity of at least four hours of weekly sport (DCMS 2008).

Widening participation will help to identify the next generation of potential elite performers at an early stage, but DCMS also has other less obvious goals in mind. They claim that continued participation in sport from an early age will lead to a more active population and that this will help to address the problem of increasing levels and frequency of obesity and so reduce the risk of coronary heart disease, stroke, type 2 diabetes and certain types of cancer. Clearly, the benefits of sport to the nation are not simply about medal tables and championships.

Source: Dobson, C. (2010) *Sport and the Nation.*

Putting it all together in your essay

This final section of Part A reviews the process of using sources and looks at how to integrate quotation, paraphrase and summary into an essay paragraph. It also gives you some final comments and advice on avoiding plagiarism, and a practice exercise to help you become more aware of integrating sources into your writing.

Throughout Part A we have used extracts from the business ethics essay as examples of how to use sources, and below is a another colour-coded extract from the essay as a final example. Notice the paragraph's sequence of black – blue – black, representing the pattern of student point, sources used as support, and follow-up student comment.

You should now be able to read the complete business ethics essay in Appendix 3 on p. 144–148 with a much clearer insight into why and how the student has used his sources.

Essay extract

My third and final reason for stating that business ethics is important is as a tool for analysis, research, study and education. As shown above, the power of organisations is increasing both nationally and globally, and the decisions business people make can have far-reaching effects. Despite this fact, managers surprisingly often have no specific training in ethics. I would argue that events such as the 2008 crash outlined above demonstrate that such training is needed, and that business ethics as a field of education and training within organisations is vital.

> Student point

The study of business ethics is also important because it provides an informed framework and source of criteria through which business behaviour can be analysed and evaluated by legal bodies and other groups in society.

> Student point

As Crouch (2011) states when discussing the political and financial power of multinational corporations, civic society now has a crucial role in analysing how these businesses behave and in criticising them and voicing concerns.

> Source used as support

Even if particular behaviour is legal at the time of an event, analysis of the activity and an explicit discussion on its impact in terms of agreed ethical standards can lead to modified or even new legislation.

> Student point

Reviewing the whole process from reading sources to writing the essay

To get an overview of how the whole process works, look at Table 1, which summarises each stage in the use of a very short section of the Svensson and Wood article, with the relevant page numbers so that you can go back and review each stage in full if you wish. This is followed by Table 2, which gives a list of the page numbers for each stage in the use of the article by Albert Carr (note that we did not look at a short reflection for the Carr article, so there is no reference to one in Table 2).

Table 1   Stages in the use of the Svensson and Wood article

Stage 1: Reading the article. Page 21
. . . it is important to see business ethics as a highly dynamic and continuous process without an end. A process, however, that is predicated on the interrelationship between business and society where each one is interdependent and responsible together for the outcomes.

Extract from: Svensson, G. and Wood, G. (2008) 'A Model of Business Ethics'
Journal of Business Ethics, 77, pp. 303–322.

Stage 2: Critically analysing the article as you read. Pages 21–22
Svensson and Wood argue strongly and clearly that business and society influence each other and are dependent on each other and have a responsibility to each other to behave ethically. However, they seem to ignore the fact that . . . Still, I think that this article is solid enough to use as one of my main sources as evidence for what I think my conclusion will probably be, which is that businesses need to have good ethics and that business ethics is important both to businesses and to society.

Stage 3: Making notes on the article. Page 28
  p.319.
A main point
  BE-'. . . dynamic and continuous process . . .' – 'interrelationship between businesses and society . . .' – each responsible for the other.

Stage 4: Writing a critical reflection of the article. Page 29
The authors propose and describe their own model of business ethics, which centres around a 'dynamic and continuous process' between business and society. They argue persuasively that business and society influence each other, are dependent on each other and have a responsibility to each other.

Stage 5: Using the article in the business ethics essay. Appendix 3, Page 146
On a more theoretical level, Svensson and Wood (2008) offer a model that shows how business and society are mutually dependent, and that both are responsible for the consequences and effects of the other as part of a dynamic two-way process.

Table 2	Stages in the use of the Carr article
Stage 1	Article extract. pp. 22–23
Stage 2	Critical analysis. Appendix 1, pp. 125–126
Stage 3	Notes. Appendix 1, pp. 126–127
Stage 5	Paraphrase in essay. Appendix 3, p. 145

Time management for each stage of the process of using your reading in your essays

Figure 1 on the next page summarises each stage of the process, and gives the approximate minimum times needed if you were searching online and using four journal articles. The precise time you will need will of course vary but it's useful to have some rough guidelines, particularly as one reason students get poor marks for their work is simply because they have not given enough time to each part of the process.

Avoiding accidental plagiarism

Common causes of both purposeful and accidental plagiarism are:

- not giving enough time to reading and understanding texts;
- not taking notes or writing a reflection;
- not understanding what counts as plagiarism in writing;
- lack of ability or confidence in restating something using your own words;
- not wanting to highlight the fact that you have used lots of sources;
- not giving clear in-text referencing;
- writing an essay that consists almost entirely of sources (even if they are all correctly referenced).

Part A of this book has taken you through key steps and practice exercises that address each of the issues listed above. The Part A sections have hopefully helped you to understand what plagiarism is, and given you the knowledge and confidence to use your sources properly and effectively. Plagiarising will not do anything to help you learn and will not help you gain the skills you need for your future career. Even if your goal at university is only to get good marks, plagiarising is still a waste of time because it almost always results in poor-quality work. It is in fact easier, more enjoyable, and a better strategy for getting good marks, to do the work needed to produce your own essay.

Thinking; thoughts and ideas on the essay title.	Thinking	Finding and selecting four relevant texts. Recording research details.	Thinking	Reading, questioning, evaluating and locating the texts in the subject	Thinking	Re-reading and making clear and meaningful notes.	Thinking	Writing a critical reflection from your notes on each text that includes whether/how the texts have developed or changed your argument.	Thinking	Deciding precisely why and how you want to use the texts as support in your argument.	Thinking	Paraphrasing, summarising and quoting the texts as part of writing your draft essay.	Thinking	Checking that your sources precisely support your points, that you have used your own words and style, and that you have given in-essay references.
		1–2 hours		4 hours		2–3 hours		2 hours		1 hour		1 hour		1 hour

Figure 1 Time management for using your reading in your essay

A useful metaphor: building a house

When thinking about originality and avoiding plagiarism, you might find it helpful to think of the essay writing process in terms of designing and building a house (the house is your essay and the materials and fittings are your sources).

The first thing you would need to do is to be clear about the purpose of the house; why you were building it and what requirements you wanted it to meet. Even if you had been given the basic design and requirements of the house (the essay title), you would still need to think about exactly how to meet the specifications of the design.

The materials for building the house (your sources) would need to be well researched, reliable and right for the job. The different materials and fittings you would use would mainly be ones that someone else had produced, but the house would be original to you because of your design features, which materials and fittings you had decided to use and how you had decided to use them. You would also keep receipts and manufacturer's details (a research log) in case of any problems and for use on future building projects.

When you had finished your house and were showing people round (anyone who reads your essay) they would be interested in who had designed and made various fittings such as the windows or kitchen units. You would hopefully be proud to answer their questions honestly. No-one would expect you to have made the kitchen units or windows yourself (and it would be obvious to anyone with any building experience that you had not done so). What *would* be important would be showing your intelligence and skill in finding and selecting the right materials, understanding how they worked, and using them effectively in your own way to build your own house that meets the design brief.

Eight Key points to remember about using your reading in your essays

- Your tutors want to see that you have been able to discriminate between different sources and select the most relevant ones.
- It is essential that you become really familiar with what you read so that you have a clear and independent understanding of it. Your tutors also want to see that you have been able to use and integrate your sources appropriately in your essay.
- You should read with a purpose in mind, but also be prepared to modify or change your viewpoint as a result of how your thinking develops as you read.
- Get the best marks possible for your work by always giving in-essay references so that your tutor can distinguish your ideas from those of your sources. Referencing all your sources also makes your work more credible and therefore more persuasive.
- An effective use of quotation, paraphrase and summary will enable you to control your sources and make them work for you in your essay.
- Never use a source without commenting on it in some way.
- Everyone approaches writing differently, and there is not one correct way to write an essay. It is important that you care about your writing and that you feel it is your own individual piece of work. Even if you use lots of sources, as long as you reference them, your essay will still be original because of which sources you have used, how you have analysed and evaluated them and how you have used them to support your argument and your individual answer to the assignment question.
- Skills and confidence and in quoting, paraphrasing and summarising will come with practice.

Practice 11: what do you think of the way these students have used this source in their essay?

Below are three paragraphs from three separate essays addressing the title: 'In what ways might personality affect job satisfaction?'

All three students have used the Robinson text on p. 48–49. Re-read the Robinson text and then read the three essay paragraphs to decide what the problem is in each case, then read the comments on each paragraph.

Finally, look at the example of a good paragraph in which the student has used their notes and reflection on the text as a basis for integrating the source information into their essay.

Unacceptable essay paragraphs

1 There does seem to be a link between personality and job satisfaction, although there are different views on how strong this link is. One interesting study on emotion regulation has demonstrated that there is a strong link between how we regulate our emotions at work and how satisfied we are with our jobs (Cote and Morgan 2002, cited in Robinson 2011). Their data showed that the amplification of pleasant emotions happened more frequently than the suppression of unpleasant emotions. Importantly, they also found a strong correlation between emotion regulation and job satisfaction and intention to quit. These finding would suggest that if you are good at regulating your emotions and particularly if you are able to be (or at least pretend to be) positive, you are likely to have a higher level of job satisfaction than someone who cannot or does not want to amplify positive emotions. Although emotion regulation is not synonymous with personality, it seems likely that personality type is linked to emotion regulation and therefore to job satisfaction.

2 There does seem to be a link between personality and job satisfaction, although there are different views on how strong this link is. A study has shown that there is a strong link between how we regulate our emotions at work and how satisfied we are with our jobs. Workers exaggerate positive emotions more than they hide negative feelings. In addition, suppressing negative emotions leads to less job satisfaction and amplifying positive emotions leads to better social interaction at work and therefore more job satisfaction. If you are good at regulating your emotions and particularly if you are able to be (or at least pretend to be) positive, you are likely to have a higher level of job satisfaction than someone who cannot or does not want to amplify positive emotions. Although emotion regulation is not synonymous with personality, it seems likely that personality type is linked to emotion regulation and therefore to job satisfaction (Cote and Morgan 2002, cited in Robinson 2011).

3 Cote and Morgan claim that there is a strong link between emotion regulation and job satisfaction and intention to quit (Cote and Morgan 2002, cited in Robinson 2011). The findings showed that workers exaggerate positive emotions more than they hide negative feelings. Cote and Morgan also found that suppressing negative emotions leads to less job satisfaction and that amplifying positive emotions leads to better social interaction at work and therefore more job satisfaction.

Comments on the unacceptable essay paragraphs

1 This paragraph starts well, with the student introducing her own point that there is a link between personality and job satisfaction. She then starts to paraphrase the Robinson article and

gives a correct in-essay reference. However, the third and fourth sentences are copied word for word from the Robinson text without any quotation marks; this is plagiarism. The paragraph ends well with the student's own comments.

2 The student starts well by introducing her own point. She continues by summarising the Robinson text in her own words, which is good. However, she does not give any in-essay references or reference reminder phrases; this is plagiarism. After her summary she continues with her own comments on the implications of the study. At the end of the last sentence she gives an in-essay reference, even though this last sentence is her own point, not that of Cote and Morgan – this means that the student is misrepresenting the source and in addition is not getting credit for her own idea. When reading this paragraph, the tutor would not be able to see clearly which points were those of the student and which those of the source.

3 This paragraph contains only the summary of the Robinson text. There are in-essay references but there is no introduction or conclusion by the student and we therefore have no idea what point the student is trying to make. This is an example of the sources controlling the essay – the student has merely found sources she thinks might be relevant and put them in, without introducing them or thinking about what point she wants them to support in her essay.

Example of an acceptable essay paragraph using the Robinson text

There does seem to be a link between personality and job satisfaction, although there are different views on how strong this link is. | *Student point*

One interesting study on emotion regulation has demonstrated that there is a strong link between how we regulate our emotions at work, and how satisfied we are with our jobs (Cote and Morgan 2002, cited in Robinson 2011). The findings showed that workers exaggerate positive emotions more than they hide negative feelings. Cote and Morgan also found that suppressing negative feelings leads to less job satisfaction, and that amplifying positive ones leads to better social interaction at work and therefore higher job satisfaction. | *Summary of source used as evidence and support*

These findings would suggest that if you are good at regulating your emotions (and particularly if you are able to be, or at least pretend to be positive) you are likely to have a higher level of job satisfaction than someone who cannot or does not want to amplify their positive emotions. The fact that if you suppress negative feelings you will have lower job satisfaction, suggests that if you are someone who can express negative feelings in a constructive way at work in order to find a solution to the problem, you will probably have higher job satisfaction than someone who hides negative emotions without trying to resolve them. | *Student's ideas on the implications of the findings*

Although emotion regulation is not synonymous with personality, it seems likely that personality type is linked to emotion regulation and therefore to job satisfaction. | *Conclusion of student's point.*

Useful vocabulary

Introduction to Part B: key points for developing your vocabulary

To write successfully you need to be able to communicate complex ideas clearly and effectively; imprecise or incorrect word use will lessen the clarity and credibility of your work. Using words and phrases in a 'nearly but not quite right' way is a common problem in student writing and common causes include: not having a large enough vocabulary to write in a fairly formal style that is also clear and to the point; understanding a word when read but not well enough for precise use in writing; and getting the main word right but making a mistake with the words that come before or after it. Part B gives you vocabulary and word information that will help you avoid all of these pitfalls and use your sources in your writing with clarity and precision.

Use Part B as a resource to refer to as and when you need, and do the practice exercises that are most useful to you. Grammar points are explained only when necessary.

Each section in Part B will give you:

- approximately 200 key words and phrases frequently used in academic writing for introducing, discussing, integrating, and evaluating sources in your work.[1] The key words and phrases are underlined and given in the context of a sentence taken from good academic writing;
- brief definitions and key points on words that are often used incorrectly by students;
- examples of student sentences that contain common vocabulary errors for you to correct, using words presented earlier in that section;
- further practice in using vocabulary in a precise way. Answers and explanatory notes for the practice exercises are given in Appendix 1, pp. 129–134.

Why use more formal vocabulary?

Academic texts and student writing usually use a fairly formal style and vocabulary. The collection of words and phrases used across most academic disciplines is often called 'common academic vocabulary' and this style is accepted and understood by scholars, students and other readers across the globe. In addition to this vocabulary, each discipline has its own specialised words, terminology and style variations.

---

1 Parts of sections B2 to B5 use adapted extracts from Godfrey J (2013) *The Student Phrase Book*, Palgrave Macmillan. See *The Student Phrase Book* for more words and phrases to in use in your academic writing.

It is important to be able to understand common academic vocabulary because academic texts use a high proportion of such words, and because although your tutors will explain discipline-specific vocabulary to you, they will expect you to understand the more common academic vocabulary as a matter of course.

If you are not familiar with formal academic writing style it can be difficult at first to judge just how formal to be. Remember that it is more important to be authentic and to explain things clearly than to try to use lots of 'long words', and that you should never try to use words you don't understand. Be aware also that some published books and articles use a style that is too complex and formal, and are, in fact, poorly written.

To sum up, although you should definitely not try to be over-complicated, you do need to understand and use fairly formal words and phrases.

A dictionary will give you information about the formality of a word. If a word entry has one of the following labels next to it, it is not appropriate to use in an academic context: *inf.* (meaning *informal*), *dated, archaic, poetic/literary, rare, humorous, euphemistic, dialect, offensive, vulgar, slang, derogatory*. Words that have no label or that are labelled as formal are appropriate to use in your academic writing. Section B7 gives examples of word and phrases students sometimes use but that are inappropriate because they are too informal or speech-like for academic writing.

Developing your vocabulary

You probably already know the approximate meaning of many words commonly used in academic writing. You therefore need to practise using the words you know more precisely, and gradually to learn and use other new useful words and phrases. Your vocabulary knowledge will increase over the time of your course and beyond, and the simple fact is that the more you read and write, the more quickly you will learn and be able to use new words precisely.

A strategy for developing your vocabulary

You will be surprised how quickly you can learn and use new words if you do some or all of the following.

1 Buy and *use* a good English-English dictionary

Online dictionaries are good, but consider buying a paper version so that you can browse through it at any time. Some dictionaries give you the key word in an example sentence and also give you useful information about the key word. If you use your dictionary effectively, it will probably prove to be one of the most useful books you buy. To get the most out of your dictionary, read the user's guide and make sure you understand the abbreviations the dictionary uses (an explanation of abbreviations is given in Appendix 5, pp. 142–153).

There are also subject-specific dictionaries to help you with the more specialised vocabulary of your discipline.

2 Read as much as possible

Research has shown that the best way to expand your vocabulary is by reading.

Academic texts frequently use common academic vocabulary, but this vocabulary set is not much used in other text types such as novels, newspapers or websites, so it is important to focus your reading on academic texts. Don't be tempted to read only easy text books or short, easy articles. Have the confidence to read short sections of more challenging books and academic journals, even if you have to read them several times and look words up – such texts will become easier to understand with practice.

3 Note down useful words

As you read, develop a sense for distinguishing between words that are useful to learn and those that are not.

Useful words are the ones that that crop up regularly in your reading. Look at the words and phrases given in Part B of this book and other books and websites that contain academic vocabulary.

Research has shown that people develop their vocabulary more quickly if they note down and group new words in an organised way, for example by topic or writing functions such as 'evaluating data' or 'suggesting implications'.

If you are reading a text in electronic format, you can use the 'find' function to highlight each time a particular word or phrase occurs so that you can see how it is commonly used in a sentence.

4 Make sure you understand what a word means and how to use it

When you learn a new word try to do the following:

- Be aware that some words have more than one meaning, and that some have different meanings depending on whether they are used in a formal or informal context. Examples of such words are *discipline* and *argument.*

- Use your dictionary to find out whether the word can be used as:

    a noun – e.g. '*Consideration* of this issue is important.'
    a verb –e.g. 'We need to *consider* this issue carefully.'
    an adjective – e.g. 'A *considerable* amount of research has been done on this issue.'
    an adverb – 'We must conduct *considerably* more research in order to understand the effects of the drug.'

- If the word is a noun, use your dictionary to find out whether it can be counted (i.e. can be both singular and plural) or is uncountable. For example, the word *consideration* can be counted. You can say 'There *is* one key *consideration*' or 'There *are several considerations* to take into account'.
    The word *research* cannot be counted. You can say 'Important research has been conducted' but you cannot say '<u>An</u> important research has been conducted' or 'Several important researc<u>hes</u> <u>have</u> been conducted'.

- Note how the word fits into a sentence (its grammar).

- Take note of any common prefixes (such as *inter-/intra-/super-/anti-/poly-/post-/pre-*) which may help you understand a word, and find out what the correct negative form of the word is. For example, The negative form of *appropriate* is <u>in</u>*appropriate*, not <u>un</u>*appropriate.*

- Use your dictionary to find out whether the key word is often or always used with other specific words. This feature of language is called collocation. For example:

    'Consideration *of* this issue is vital.'
    'This issue is currently *under consideration by* the government.'
    '*Careful consideration of* this issue is important.'
    'We need to *take into consideration* the long term effects.'
    Be aware also that some words cannot be used together if one has a positive meaning and the other has a negative meaning (the connotation of the word). For example, we don't say 'There were abundant mistakes' because *abundant* has a positive meaning and is not used to describe something negative such as mistakes.

- Try to find out if there are words that have a similar meaning (a synonym) or an opposite meaning (an antonym) to the key word. This will help you to build up your word repertoire, and knowledge of synonyms will enable you to avoid being too repetitive in your writing. Remember though, that many synonyms are close rather than exact equivalents of the key word.

5 *Use* the words you have learnt

Understanding what words mean is not enough; you need to practise *using* these words accurately.

Reading and writing are two sides of the same coin – using words confidently can only come with practice, so get into the habit of writing something every day – for example, a short summary or rephrasing or critique of something you have read, your thoughts and ideas on what you have read, a study journal, or a draft paragraph of an assignment.

6 Be authentic

Never use a word you don't understand. Your tutor would much rather see you explain your ideas in more simple, informal words than use more formal words incorrectly.

7 Use feedback

Reflecting and taking action on the feedback you get from tutors will help you to improve your written work.

Introducing sources and using verbs precisely

In Section A7 we looked at how to integrate your sources into your assignment. Section B1 looks first at different ways of introducing a source into your essay and then looks at an important area of vocabulary for introducing, reporting and evaluating your sources; using verbs precisely.

Three different ways of introducing and referring to your source

1 Emphasising the information

If you wish to emphasise the idea or information in your source rather than the author, you can quote, paraphrase or summarise the information and only give the in-essay reference at the end of the sentence in round brackets (or use a number at the end of the sentence if you are using numeric referencing). For example:

> 'Although the law overlaps with ethics, it usually only regulates the lowest level of acceptable behaviour (Crane and Matten 2010).'

2 Emphasising the information and the research

If you wish to refer in a general way to the fact that research or other work has been done, mention this fact but again only give the specific reference at the end of the sentence in round brackets. This technique emphasises the information and the research or studies which have been done, rather than specific authors. This technique is useful for bringing together similar research or work and for referencing several authors together. Note that for this type of general reporting, the verb is usually used in the present perfect tense. For example:

> '<u>Research has indicated </u>that job satisfaction is linked to regulating emotion (Cote and Morgan 2002, Barrick 2002).'

You can also use the passive tense (with or without the 'by + agent' phrase). For example:

> '<u>It has been suggested that</u> violent films have a negative effect on children's behaviour (Carlton 1999; Cyprian 2001).'
> 'This idea of the interdependence of any business organisation is also supported by Shaw and Barry (2007), Green (1994), Fritzsche (2005) and Svensson and Wood (2008).'

3 Emphasising the author

If you wish to emphasise the specific author/s of the source, give the author as part of your sentence, with only the year of publication in round brackets (or give a number after the author's name if you are using numeric referencing). You can use this method when you want to show that you have reviewed the literature and that you know who the key authors are, and which of them hold similar views to each other. For example:

> 'Svensson and Wood (2008) show that the two are in fact mutually dependent . . .'
> 'Others such as Wolf (2008) share this view, and Prindl and Prodham (1994) suggest that . . .'

Using verbs precisely

When we use verbs to report on and describe what someone else has said or done, we refer to them as *reporting verbs* (although we also use many of these verbs to give our own views, evaluations and to develop our own arguments). It is important to use these verbs precisely when you quote, paraphrase or summarise a source. Notice that in method 1 above, reporting verbs are not used because the source is not explicitly mentioned as part of the sentence. In methods 2 and 3 however, reporting verbs (*indicate, suggest, support, show* and *share*) are needed.

Key points for using verbs

1 Choose an appropriate verb to show that you understand what the author is doing

In academic writing we do not use the verbs *say* or *tell* because they are too vague and speech-like. To describe what an author is doing (without necessarily saying whether you agree or disagree with them) you need to be precise in your use of reporting verbs such as *argue, discuss, examine, explain, give, state, suggest, trace, question*. Each verb has a different meaning and it is important to use the right one in order to show your reader that you understand what the author is doing. For example:

> 'Mepham (2006) <u>questions</u> the method of 'learning' bioethics and <u>states</u> that a critical approach is fundamental to this field of enquiry.'
> 'Musssen et al. (1956) were one of the first teams to <u>trace</u> the development of a child's personality from birth to adulthood.'
> 'Lobstein et al. <u>justify</u> their recommendation to use the traffic-light system of food labelling by . . .'

2 Choose an appropriate verb to show that you understand the content of the source

Verbs commonly used to report what an author does in their text are ones such as <u>establish, prove, show, demonstrate, investigate,</u> and <u>identify</u>. Make sure that you choose a verb that is correct for the relevant object or noun; you can't <u>discover</u> an experiment or <u>argue</u> a question – you <u>conduct</u> an experiment and <u>address, discuss</u> or <u>examine</u> a question.

3 Choose an appropriate verb to show that you understand the author's viewpoint

Authors often give their views in a text and comment on the views of others, so make sure that you use a verb which reports this correctly. For example, if you want to express the fact that one author does not agree with something or someone, you would use verbs such as <u>question, query, challenge, dispute, reject</u> or <u>deny.</u> For example:

> 'Carr (1968) <u>challenges</u> the assumption that when managers talk about good ethics they are expressing a true desire to behave well.'

4 Choose an appropriate verb to show *your* viewpoint

You can also use reporting verbs as a powerful tool for showing *your* attitude to a source and for showing how a source supports your own argument. For example, look at the sentence below taken directly from an article by Deborah Lupton 1998 entitled 'Medicine and Health Care in Popular Media'.

'Research would certainly suggest that the lay public has a strong interest in health and medical issues in the media'.

If you want to agree with Lupton in your essay, you might report what she says using a 'positive' verb such as <u>establish, show, demonstrate, identify, note, inform, confirm, observe, point out, prove, illustrate</u> or <u>reveal.</u> For example:

> i) 'Lupton (1998) <u>shows that</u> people are very interested in stories and news about medical and health matters.'

However, if you wanted to argue against Lupton and say that the public does not have an interest in health and medicine in the media, you would need to report Lupton in your essay using a neutral verb and then give a comment indicating that you disagree with her and that you think what she says is questionable or wrong.

> ii) 'Lupton (1998) <u>asserts that</u> people are very interested in stories and news about medical and health matters but this idea seems to be contradicted by later studies.'

Neutral verbs that can be used in this way are: <u>assert, assume, claim, maintain, argue, suggest</u> and <u>state</u>. For example:

> 'Morris <u>states that</u> her work on euthanasia is informed by a feminist perspective. However, it is not clear how this helps the debate in any meaningful way.'

5 Match the attitude of subsequent sentences to that of your reporting verb

Make sure that the attitude of subsequent sentences matches that of the verb you have used to report your source. For example, which of sentence (a) and (b) below should follow sentences (i) and (ii) above?

a) 'Moreover, I would argue that having a large amount of media coverage given to such issues does not necessarily demonstrate that we are really interested in them.'

b)   'Indeed, some of the most popular current TV shows are hospital dramas.'

6 Use the correct grammatical structure with your verb

In the active tense all verbs need to be used with one or more of the following grammatical structures:

- Verb + that + clause.
  For example: 'Lupton <u>asserts that the public is interested in medical stories</u>.'
- Verb + what / why / where / who / whether + clause.
  For example: 'Lockhart (2009) <u>discusses whether advertising reinforces stereotypes</u>.'
- Verb + infinitive.
  For example: 'Keil's report <u>aims to cover</u> all aspects of government policy.'
- Verb + noun (object).
  For example: 'Dawkins <u>regards religious education</u> as a form of indoctrination.'
- Verb + -ing form (object).
  For example: 'Dawkins <u>regards teaching</u> religion as a form of indoctrination.'
- Verb + object + infinitive.
  For example: 'The study <u>encourages us to ask</u> whether wealth distribution is desirable.'
- Verb + object + preposition +-ing.
  For example: 'Gould <u>accuses Dawkins of pandering</u> to "middle of the road religious people"'.

Some verbs can be used with more than one grammatical structure. For example:

Lupton	<u>shows that</u>	the public is very interested in medical stories.
Lin and Moon	<u>show why</u>	the public is very interested in medical stories.
The study	<u>shows the link</u>	between folklore and history.

However, most reporting verbs are commonly used in only one or two of the above structures. Note that some verbs cannot be followed by *that* and must be followed by a noun/object. For example:

'The novel graphically <u>portrays that</u> the horrors of the First World War.' ✘
'The novel graphically <u>portrays</u> the horrors of the First World War.' ✔
'The article essay <u>discusses that</u> the UK and American legal systems are similar.' ✘
'The article <u>discusses</u> the similarities between the UK and American legal system.' ✔

When you are reading, try to notice how reporting verbs are commonly used and use your dictionary to help you identify the correct grammatical structure/s for particular verbs.

7 Be aware that you may need to use two or more verbs

Authors will often do more than one thing in their text, so you may often need two or more verbs. For example:

'Cote and Morgan <u>conducted</u> two studies and <u>demonstrated that</u> there is a link between regulating emotions and job satisfaction.'

8. Be consistent in your use of tense

When referring to a source it is common to use the present simple tense although you can also use the past simple, as long as you are consistent. For example:

> 'Bergl and Vigilant (2006) <u>provide</u> important data on the migration patterns of the Cross River gorilla.'
> 'Bergl and Vigilant (2006) <u>provided</u> important data on the migration patterns of the Cross River gorilla.'

However, if the material is quite old or if you are referring to a particular study, it is more common to use the simple past. For example:

> 'Gurtman's study (1990) <u>showed</u> that unconscious ageism has an impact on people's behaviour.'
> 'In his 1905 paper Einstein <u>presented</u> the theory of special relativity.'

If you are referring to several authors, studies or research in general, the present perfect tense is usually used. For example:

> 'Several studies (Cote and Morgan 2002, Barrick 2002) have shown that job satisfaction is linked to regulating emotion.'

Practice 12: error correction

Below are student sentences that contain errors (given in italics) in how the reporting verbs have been used.

Sentences 1–9 use the wrong verb and 10–12 use the correct verb but with the wrong grammatical structure. Correct the sentences. Answers and comments are given on p. 130.

1 Researchers in the UK are *undergoing studies about* the possible effects of the drug.
2 There is much evidence to *clarify* just how harmful cigarettes are.
3 Corson *imposed* that there are two main styles of English.
4 To summarise Karlov's argument, he *mentions* that playing chess uses a similar part of the brain as playing music.
5 The idea of using a computer program to collectively edit a website was *perceived* by Cunningham and Beck in the late 1990s.
6 The telephone was *established* by Alexander Bell.
7 The ideas *portrayed* in the report are not new.
8 As i*mplied* by Murtaz (2007), 'patient care should be the primary motive for developments in the NHS' (p. 1).
9 Laurent (2007) *claims* that 'genetic engineering is the most important advance in medicine since the development of vaccines' (p. 15). This essay will demonstrate that this is clearly the case.
10 Lupton *discusses about* the portrayal of medicine and health in the media.
11 This essay will *argue a link* between regulating emotions and job satisfaction.
12 Emotion regulation is *defined that* you hide or try to modify your emotions.

Describing the views of different authors

Describing an author's position and views

When you are using sources to help develop your own argument, you will need to understand, describe and analyse the various viewpoints of the source authors. Below are some example sentences and word information for vocabulary to describe the position an author takes and to describe viewpoints in general.

In the example sentences the key words and phrases are underlined, with words that have similar meanings separated by a / and words that have different meanings but that can be used in the same sentence structure separated by //.

Position

- The article criticises the government's <u>stance / position</u> on potential strike action.
- Increasingly, schools are <u>positioning</u> themselves <u>within</u> a free market economy.
- The book looks at the medieval Christian crusades <u>from the perspective of</u> the Muslim world.
- Personal blogs are written from a purely subjective <u>standpoint.</u>
- The study looks at salt sensitivity in the Japanese population <u>from the viewpoint of</u> genetic diversity.

Points of view

- It is important to analyse the facts before <u>formulating a view.</u>
- <u>The view that</u> all research should be concerned with developing theory <u>is</u> debatable, according to May (2000).
- Bellamy's essay <u>takes the view that</u> earning money from money is unethical.
- Baldini <u>thinks / holds the opinion / is of the opinion</u> that using animals for experimentation is inhumane.
- Picasso <u>is</u> widely <u>regarded as / viewed as / thought of as / considered to be</u> a major influence in twentieth century art.

Views that agree, support, argue for or accept

- There <u>is</u> cross-party <u>agreement on</u> the issue of identification cards.
- Patel is a <u>proponent of / advocate of / supporter of</u> civil liberties in the UK.
- The health centre <u>endorses</u> homeopathy.
- Smith is a leading <u>exponent</u> of permaculture and runs related workshops across the country.
- Research literature supports the idea that a successful organization is one that <u>embraces</u> change.

- Diehm and Armatas (2004) look at how surfing is a high-risk activity that has been <u>accepted by</u> society.
- Penrose <u>admits / acknowledges / concedes / accepts that</u> producing a unified theory is a long-term endeavour.
- The poll showed that 61 per cent of Americans <u>condoned</u> capital punishment in cases of murder.
- <u>The argument for</u> intelligent design is that biological structures are too complex to have arisen via an undirected process.

Views that disagree or oppose

- The main <u>objections</u> to the airport proposal are noise, nuisance and damage to wildlife habitat.
- Nativists <u>object to</u> the idea that we are born as 'blank slates' <u>on the grounds that</u> some beliefs are genetically programmed.
- Dawkins <u>is opposed to / rejects</u> the idea of faith schools.
- The Unionists are <u>against / averse to</u> the idea of Ireland being independent from the UK.
- <u>Opponents of</u> stem cell research argue that there is no moral justification for using and destroying embryonic cells.

Counterarguments and alternative viewpoints

- <u>An argument against / An argument that counters / A counterargument to</u> the idea of evolution is that life is too complex to have developed without intelligent direction.
- <u>A challenge to</u> pro-capitalism ideology is that it inevitably results in the rich getting richer and the poor getting poorer.
- <u>An alternative view / A challenge to this point of view</u> is that capitalism is 'the greatest tool of ... social advance ever known...'.

Useful information on some of these words

advocate *v./n.*   Definition: *v.* – To actively support.
n. – A (strong) supporter of something.
Common phrases:
An **advocate of / for** X.
To **actively // openly // strongly advocate** X.

averse *adj.*   Definition: Opposed to.
Commonly confused: *Averse* and *adverse*
Adverse means unpleasant and/or harmful.

condone *v.*   Definition: To accept or (reluctantly) agree with or approve of behaviour usually viewed as morally wrong.
Common phrases: To condone **behaviour // the practice of // the action of // violence // abuse // torture // murder**.

counter *v.*   Definition: To respond with an opposing argument, view or action.

Common phrases:
To counter **a claim // an argument // a threat // a criticism // fundamentalism // terrorism // extremism**.

counterargument *n.*   Definition: An argument that opposes another argument.
Commonly confused: *counterargument* and *counterclaim*
In academic writing you can counter a claim someone makes. However, the noun and verb *counterclaim* are usually reserved for legal or insurance contexts. For example, after a car crash, the car owner claims for damages and the other person then counterclaims (or make a counterclaim) for personal injury.

embrace *v.*   Definition: To accept and welcome something.
Common phrases:
To **willingly // actively // wholeheartedly // fully** embrace.
To embrace (a) **change // challenge // concept / notion / idea // opportunity**.

endorse *v.*   Definition: *v.* – To publicly support and recommend an idea, belief,
endorsement *n.*   action or product.

exponent *n.*   Definition: (1) (Of people) an example, practitioner or representative (and so also probably a supporter) of something. (2) A skilled artist or performer, usually a musician.
Commonly confused: *exponent* and *proponent*
See under *proponent* below.

perspective *n.*   Definition: (1) A particular mental position or way of thinking from which a view on a specific issue is formed.
For example: I will discuss personal identity from a social behaviourist perspective.
Similar to *position*, *standpoint* and *viewpoint*.
(2) Representing three-dimensional space on a two-dimensional surface.

proponent *n.*   Definition: Someone who puts forward or is in favour of a plan, idea or theory. Similar to *advocate* and *supporter*.
Commonly confused: *proponent* and *exponent*
The two words are sometimes used interchangeably but there is a difference in meaning.
A proponent is in favour of an idea but does not necessarily make their support public or act on it (often because the idea or theory is not something they can practically do).
An exponent is in favour of something but, more importantly, does something about it.

stance *n.*   Definition: A clear position on something.
Common phrases: A **hard-line / tough // firm // ethical // moral** stance on X.

To **have // adopt // hold // take** a stance **on / against** X.

view *v./n.*

Definition: *n.* – An opinion, belief or attitude, often not based on evidence.

v. – (1) To think of in a particular way.

(2) To look at or inspect. This is formal use of *view*.

For example: We viewed the landscape through binoculars.

Common phrases:

A **personal // broad // narrow // simplistic // orthodox // traditional** view.

To **subscribe to / hold a particular** view.

X **reflects the view that** . . .

viewpoint *n.*

Definition: A particular way of thinking about something. Similar to *standpoint* and *perspective.*

Common phrases:

A(n) **alternative // different // alternative // opposing // subjective // objective** viewpoint.

Commonly confused: *viewpoint, view* and *point of view.* These words are often are used interchangeably but strictly speaking, a *viewpoint* is a more general position from which a specific view / point of view is formed.

Practice 13: error correction

Below are ten sentences from real student essays. The sentences are nearly but not quite right (errors are in italics) because the student has used the wrong word, or used the right word but with incorrect form or grammar. Use the examples and word information above to correct the sentences. Answers are given on p. 130.

1 There are several *disagreements* as to what constitutes an offence.
2 Brenner is a strong *advocate in* women's rights.
3 A primary *argument* of some religious groups to IVF is that it uses external fertilisation.
4 Balkin (2002) *oppose* to sex segregation in schools in that it is a diversion from more important educative issues.
5 Many pressure groups have strong *views* against embryonic research.
6 Some people see *it* as since they already pay income tax, they should not be additionally taxed on interest from savings.
7 This report has outlined the factors that *condemn against* animal testing.
8 Mueller (2011) states that people often *refute* creative ideas because they are scared of change.
9 The current government in Mexico is adopting an expansionary economic *view*.
10 A *counterclaim* to humour being used to show dominance is that it is used to relieve social tension.

Comparing the views of different authors and showing how they cite and evaluate each other

For most essays you will need to discuss your sources in relation to each other, showing how the views of different authors are similar or different. Below are some example sentences and word information that give you vocabulary for comparing sources that have similar, different or diverging views and information, and words and phrases for expressing contrast. Some of the example sentences have been adapted from sentences in the business ethics essay and other extracts from Part A.

In the example sentences, the key words or phrases are underlined, with words that have similar meanings separated by a / and words that have different meanings but that can be used in the same sentence structure separated by //.

Example sentences

Similar and convergent views

- <u>Both</u> Marteinson <u>and</u> Bergson view humour as arising from conflict between the real and the unreal.
- Cote and Morgan <u>are in agreement with / agree with / share the same view as / hold a similar view to</u> Hoschild, that is, that suppressing emotions can cause stress in employees.
- Cote and Morgan, <u>together with</u> Hoschschild, hold the view that suppressing emotions can cause stress in workers.
- <u>Neither</u> Wolf <u>nor</u> Carr feels that businesses should concern themselves with ethics.
- Both articles show <u>considerable overlap in</u> how they view the link between literacy and reasoning.
- There is <u>overlap / common ground between</u> the two authors, as they both view humour as arising from…
- Collins' and Esty's positions <u>converge</u> on the issue of business and social responsibility.

Different and divergent views

- Clint and others maintain that humour is used to assert superiority. <u>However,/ In contrast, / On the other hand,</u> Berlyne proposes that humour serves to relieve tension.
- Clint and others maintain that humour is used to assert superiority. Berlyne, <u>however, / in contrast, / on the other hand,</u> proposes that humour serves to relieve tension.

- Whereas / Although Wolf believes that business operate separately from society, Wood shows that the two are mutually dependent.
- Wolf suggests that business should operate separately from society, while / whereas Wood shows that they are interdependent.
- Wolf states that business and society should act separately from each other, but opponents of this view suggest that the two are co-dependent.
- There are diverse / varied / different opinions as to whether ethics do have a valid place in a business.
- The literature reveals two different / distinct / discrete theories.
- Although both Miller and Hurley agree that humour is connected to sexual selection, they disagree on / their views differ in regard to / they diverge on the extent of the role humour plays.
- Miller's view differs from that of Hurley's as to the degree of importance humour has in evolutionary selection.

Describing how one source cites another as support and/or comments positively

- Barrick et al. (2002) cite Bakan as a proponent of the idea that achieving status is a key goal in social interaction.
- Halle quotes from Le Corbusier (1986) as support for his argument that abstract art has been idealised in art theory.
- Hepner paraphrases / uses paraphrases from // quotes from / uses quotations from the Bible as justification for his ideas.
- Hepner uses Bible extracts / excerpts (in an attempt) to defend / justify his ideas.
- According to Woolf, Austen made a great contribution to fiction, despite not having a private writing space.
- Woolf acknowledged Austen's contribution to fiction and the fact that she wrote despite not having any private space.
- Jung credited Gross with having preceded him in identifying two distinct types of consciousness.

Describing how sources challenge and/or respond to each other

- According to Phillipson (2000), Crystal has a Eurocentric view of English as a global language.
- Crystal (2000) responds to / replies to Phillipson's criticism by stating that he merely describes how English is used.
- Svensson and Wood (2007) disagree with / contest / refute Friedman's claim that businesses do not need to consider social issues and state that on the contrary, businesses have an enormous impact on society.
- Ainsworth counters / rebuts Dawkins' claim that faith schools are discriminatory by proposing / with the proposition / by maintaining / by asserting that such schools allow children informed choice.
- Guthrie and Parker (1989) offer a rebuttal of Legitimacy Theory. They suggest that…
- Lupton (1998) challenges / questions Fox's suggestion that doctors are no longer seen as the authorities on medical issues.

- Gould is (strongly / vigorously) challenged by Dawkins, who accuses him of writing for 'middle of the road religious people'.
- Phillipson has criticised linguists such as Crystal for having a Eurocentric view of the global dominance of English.
- Smith's main criticism of Dawkins' position is that he overstates the role religion plays in human conflict.
- Watson and Crick failed to credit Franklin in their initial publication on the structure of DNA.

Information on some of these words

according to *prep*
Definition: 'As stated by'
NB Use *according to* only when referring to other people or organisations. It is incorrect to say 'According to me . . .'

acknowledge *v.*
Definition: (1) To accept or admit something, or to show gratitude for something.
(2) In academic writing, *to acknowledge* can mean to reference/cite an author, i.e. to give their name and details of publication.

assert *v.*
Definition: To state something clearly and confidently (with or without evidence).

cite *v.*
Definition: To refer to someone or something else, either by quotation, paraphrase or name only.
NB Use *cite* only to describe when one author mentions another. It is incorrect to say 'I cite . . .'.
Commonly confused: *cite*, *site* and *sight*. Note the different spellings of these three different words.

contest *n./v.*
Definition: *v.* – To argue against a statement. Similar to *refute* and *rebut*.
To contest the **claim // suggestion // accusation // idea // theory** that . . .

converge *v.*
convergence *n.*
convergent *adj.*
Definition: *v.* – To come together (or to start to come together) from different directions / points.

counter *v.*
Definition: To respond with an opposing argument, view or action.
NB To say that 'X **is counter to** Y' or 'X **runs counter to** Y' has the slightly different meaning of an action that purposely or perhaps accidentally goes against something else.
For example: 'Building on this site would run counter to the government's policy of maintaining green spaces.'

Common phrases: To counter **a claim // an argument // a threat // a criticism // fundamentalism // terrorism // extremism.**

diverge *v.*
divergence *n.*
divergent *adj.*

Definition: *v.* –To go (or to start to go) in different directions. Usually used to describe things that start from a similar point but that then separate, or to describe things that have some similarities but also some differences.

excerpt *n.*

Definition: A short section from a book, film or piece of music. Similar to *an extract.*
Commonly confused: *excerpt* and *exert*
These two words sound the same but have different spellings and meanings.
To exert means to put pressure on someone or to make an effort to do something.

extract *n./v.*

Definition: *n.* – (1) A short section from a book, film or piece of music. Similar to *excerpt.*
(2) A concentrated food or chemical preparation.
e.g. 'Use of bitter orange extract is regulated in the US by the FDA.'
v. – (1) To remove or take something out of something else (often using force).
E.g. 'We extracted DNA from each cell.' 'The dentist extracted two teeth.'

maintain *v.*

Definition: *Maintain* has several different meanings. In the context of evaluating sources, it means to state something clearly and confidently (with or without evidence).
Similar to *claim.*

paraphrase *v./n.*

Definition: To express the meaning of writing or speech using different words, often in order to clarify or simplify. (See section A5.)

quote *v.*
quotation *n.*

Definition: *v.* – To use the exact words of someone else. (See section A4.)
NB It is incorrect to say 'I quote . . .' or 'Smith quotes that . . .' to introduce a quotation. because *quote* is usually only used to describe when one source quotes another.
For example: 'Smith quotes Robinson: "Job satisfaction is. . . ."'
Commonly confused: *quote / quotation* and *cite / citation.*
Citation is sometimes used to mean *quotation.* However, a citation can also refer to any type of reference to a source, including paraphrase or just the name of the author.

rebut *v.*
rebuttal *n.*

Definition: *v.* – To argue against a statement. Similar to *contest* and *refute* but less commonly used.

refute *v.*
refutation *n.*

Definition: To oppose a statement and, importantly, to try to prove that the statement is false.

Similar to *contest* and *rebut*.

Common phrases: To refute the **claim // suggestion // accusation // idea // theory**

reject *v./n.*

Definition: *v.* – To not accept.

Commonly confused: *reject, refute* and *deny*.

Reject has the more general meaning.

To refute is a more formal word used only in the context of argument and ideas. It differs from both *reject* and *deny* because *refute* must include giving reasons for not accepting a statement.

To deny often means to reject an accusation or the truth of something and is not usually appropriate in an academic context.

Practice 14: error correction

Below are ten sentences from real student essays. The sentences are nearly but not quite right (errors are in italics) because the student has used the wrong word, or used the right word but with incorrect form or grammar. Use the examples and word information above to correct the sentences. Answers are given on p. 131.

1 *According to me*, the issue of global warming is not as serious as the media portrays.
2 Kerlinger (1969) *quotes* that 'Science is a misused and misunderstood word' (p. 1127).
3 It has been *alleged* that computer games can be used to educate children.
4 Smith (2009) has criticised Ramone's work *as* being overcomplicated.
5 Karl Marx *refuted* capitalism as a positive system for social development.
6 According to Gilchrist, *he suggests that* we need to re-evaluate how we perceive risk-taking heroines, particularly those who are also mothers.
7 Kroll *states* Frie as an example of how early approaches to second-language learning saw teaching writing as a secondary to speech.
8 The research team *knowledge* that their data is incomplete and that further studies are needed.
9 According to (*Dr Reynolds, 2000*) there is no strong evidence of long-term damage to health.
10 As Collins (1994) *cites*, 'good ethics is synonymous with good management.' (p. 2).

Practice 15: synthesising sources

Below are brief summaries of three different theories of job satisfaction. Imagine that these are your summaries and that you now wish to combine them into one paragraph that briefly compares the three theories. Write this paragraph using vocabulary from this section, rewording, reordering and synthesising your summaries as necessary. An example paragraph is given on p. 131.

Summaries

1 Locke 's theory states that what a person wants to do in a job (their 'conscious goals and intentions') and how far these goals are achieved, are the main factors that determine job satisfaction (Locke, 1968).
2 The dispositional approach sees a person's disposition as the most important element in determining their level of job satisfaction, regardless of the job type (Staw, Bell and Clausen, 1986).
3 The most complex model proposes that organisational structure influences the characteristics of a job, and that jobs with particular characteristics attract people with particular personality attributes. These attributes determine how satisfied a person will be with their job (Oldham and Hackman, 1981) and therefore both job type and employee personality are central to determining job satisfaction.

References

Locke, E. A. (1968) 'Towards a theory of task motivation and incentives' *Organisational Behaviour and Human Performance*, 3(2), pp. 157–189.

Oldham, G. and Hackman, J. (1981) 'Relationships Between Organisational Structure and Employee Reactions: Comparing Alternative Frameworks' *Administrative Science Quarterly*, 26(1), pp. 66–83.

Staw, B., Bell, N. and Clausen, J. (1986) 'The Dispositional Approach To Job Attributes: A Lifetime Longitudinal Test' *Administrative Science Quarterly*, 31(1), pp. 56–77.

Commentating positively on a source

Below are some example sentences that give you vocabulary for introducing, describing and evaluating a source positively, i.e. in a way that shows you agree with the source and that you are using it to support your own argument.

The key words or phrases are underlined, with words that have similar meanings separated by a / and words that have different meanings but that can be used in the same sentence structure separated by //.

Useful words and phrases

Using neutral verbs to introduce a source and then give a positive comment

- Collins <u>states</u> // <u>claims / maintains</u> // <u>asserts / contends</u> that violence is a product of environmental factors. Other studies support this idea . . .
- Darwin <u>proposed / suggested</u> that individuals are 'selected' by nature over others. This idea is now well established as . . .
- Vellitino <u>examines</u> // <u>considers / takes into account</u> // <u>covers in detail</u> the four different concepts of dyslexia. He shows that . . .

Using positive verbs to comment on a source

- Milanovic (2002) <u>explains</u> how globalisation can affect income distribution. His findings are important because . . .
- Miller (1991) <u>explicates</u> the process by which people developmental models of relationships. He illustrates how . . .
- The authors <u>demonstrate / illustrate / show / establish</u> that well-run businesses are of benefit to society. Their findings . . .
- Thouless <u>observed / made the observation / noted</u> that homing pigeons do not need to know the sun's location in order to fly home.
- Skinner <u>found </u>that reinforcement strengthens patterns of behaviour.
- Perdue and Gurtman (1990) <u>identify</u> an important and previously overlooked factor in ageism, namely . . .
- Rubia investigates aspects of neuropsychology and <u>clarifies / elucidates</u> the nature of psychiatric disorders.
- The article successfully <u>simplifies</u> the complex theory of special relativity.
- Stich (1985) <u>provides</u> some illuminating examples human irrationality. The most interesting is . . .

Using positive adjectives, adverbs and nouns to comment on a source

- Plamondon gives a <u>comprehensive / thorough // extensive</u> overview of handwriting systems and offers <u>clear // useful insights</u> into . . .
- Bergl and Vigilant provide <u>important // interesting // reliable / sound</u> data on Cross River gorilla migration. Their data . . .
- The article contains <u>overwhelming // compelling // convincing // objective / hard // strong // clear // ample</u> evidence that . . .
- Their research <u>conclusively // convincingly</u> <u>shows / establishes</u> that environment affects mental health.
- In my view, Perdue and Gurtman (1990) <u>correctly</u> identify an important and previously overlooked factor in ageism, namely...
- He provides a <u>cogent // coherent / logical / sound / valid // reasonable // considered</u> argument to support his theory that . . .
- Skinner puts forward <u>innovative // convincing / persuasive / plausible / credible</u> ideas about teaching methodology.
- Stich (1985) provides some <u>illuminating examples</u> of human irrationality. The most interesting is . . .
- The report <u>benefits from</u> <u>rigorous</u> research, a <u>succinct</u> style and a <u>readable</u> format.
- <u>A clear strength of</u> the survey is the very large sample size.

Stating that source is supported by other research

- The idea proposed by Valencia-Flores et al. (2002) that the 'siesta culture' of Mexican students is a negative stereotype is <u>supported / corroborated / confirmed / verified / validated / substantiated by</u> other research in this area. Studies by . . .
- Importantly, the findings are <u>consistent with</u> those of previous studies.

Stating that a source has contributed to the field

- His <u>substantive</u> body of work has <u>influenced</u> many areas of psychology. The most important area has been . . .
- Kramer's article is a <u>noteworthy // valuable // substantive</u> <u>contribution to</u> the debate on corporate responsibility because . . .

Information on some of these words

assert *v.*	*v.* – (1) To state a fact, belief or hypothesis clearly and confidently. (2) To do something that makes others recognise your authority or right(s). Similar to *contend*.
claim *v./n.*	Definition: To state that something is the case clearly and confidently, with or without evidence. Similar to *maintain*. *v.* – To claim that . . . *n.* – To **make** a/the claim that . . .

cogent *adj.*

Definition: Logical, clear and convincing. Usually used in the context of argumentation.
Common phrases: A cogent **argument** // **case**. To **put forward / propose** a cogent argument // case.

coherent *adj.*

Definition: Logical, well-structured and consistent.
Common phrases: A coherent **argument** // **article** // **framework** // **strategy** // **policy** // **system** // **theory**.
To do X in a coherent **way / manner**.
Commonly confused : *coherent*, *cogent* and *cohesive*.
Coherent and *cogent* are often used interchangeably but strictly speaking, a coherent argument is well-structured but not necessarily cogent (convincing).
Cohesive means 'sticking together' and is usually used in the context of physical things rather than argument.
For example: 'They formed a cohesive group in order to survive.'

comprehensive *adj.*

Definition: Covering all or nearly all aspects, very wide-ranging. Similar meaning to *thorough*.
Common phrases: (A) comprehensive **review** // **examination** // **study** // **account** // **coverage** // **survey**.

conclusive *adj.*
conclusively *adv.*

Definition: *adj.* – (Of an argument or evidence) very strong and convincing.

consistent *adj.*

Definition: (1) Does not contradict.
(2) Unchanging over time.
Common phrases: A consistent **approach** // **standard** // **level**.
X is consistent with the **aim** // **data** // **evidence** / **findings** // **objective** // **principle** // **view** of Y.

contend *v.*

Definition: (1) To state a fact, belief or hypothesis clearly and confidently.
Similar to *assert*.

corroborate *v.*

Definition: To support something by giving additional data, evidence or information.
Similar to *support* except that *corroborate* is usually used for concrete evidence or empirical data rather than ideas and theories.

credible *adj.*

Definition: Authoritative and convincing.
Common phrases: A credible **source** // **evidence** // **data** // **argument** // **explanation** // **threat** // **deterrent**.
Scientifically // **politically** // **academically** credible.

elucidate *v.*

Definition: To explain and clarify.
NB *elucidate* is more formal than *explain* or *clarify*.

explicate *v.*
explication *n.*

Definition: *v.* – To analyse something in detail in order to understand its meaning and significance.
Commonly confused: *explicate* and *explain*
These words have different meanings.
To explicate means to analyse (break down and explore) something at a deep level.
For example: 'The third paragraph of this explication looks at how the poem's rhythm adds to its meaning.'
To explain means to give a description of something and/or to give the reasons why something happens or exists.
For example: 'The appendix gives an explanation of the different categories of hospital.'

extensive *adj.*

Definition: (1) Covering many aspects of an issue or idea.
For example: an extensive survey.
(2) Covering a wide area.
Commonly confused: *extensive* and *expansive*.
Expansive also means wide ranging but is used in the context of physical space (an expansive area). It also means the personal characteristic of being very communicative.
Commonly confused: *extensive* and *comprehensive*.
Extensive means covering many aspects, whereas *comprehensive* means covering all or nearly all aspects.

illuminate *v.*
illuminating *adj.*

Definition: *v.* – (1) To clarify and provide understanding and insight.
(2) To provide light.
Common phrases: An illuminating **example // discussion // piece of research // lecture // experience**.

illustrate *v.*
illustration *n.*

Definition: *v.* – (1)To give an example and/or to demonstrate.
(2)To use / provide with pictures.
Common phrases: To illustrate **a point // argument // principle // concept**.
To illustrate the/a **importance // complexity // difficulty // problem // concept // model**.
X **seeks to / attempts to / tries to // serves to** illustrate Y.

maintain *v.*

Definition: *Maintain* has several different meanings. In the context of evaluating sources, *maintain* means to state clearly and confidently that something is the case.
Similar to *claim*.

noteworthy *adj.*

Definition: Worth special attention.

plausible *adj.*

Definition: (Without evidence) seeming to be reasonable and believable.
Common phrases: A plausible **explanation // theory // argument // hypothesis // idea // interpretation**.

substantiate *v.*	Definition: To provide additional supporting evidence or information. Similar to *corroborate* and *support*.
substantive *adj.*	Definition: (1) Dealing with facts, issues and evidence (and therefore having real-world importance) rather than with theoretical concepts, formal logic or methodology. For example: Phillips (1974) looks at both the substantive and theoretical implications of the suicide data. (2) Important, main. Common phrases: A substantive **issue // body of work // report // piece of** research. Commonly confused :*substantive* and *substantial*. *Substantial* means of a large size or quantity.
succinct *adj.*	Definition: Brief and clear.
valid *adj.* **validity** *n.*	Definition: *adj.* – (1) Reasonable, well-founded and supported by evidence. (2) Logically consistent, i.e. the conclusion follows from the premise. In formal logic, an argument may be valid even though its premise and / or conclusion are untrue. For example: All birds are blue. This swan is a bird. Therefore, this swan is blue. Common phrases: **Scientifically // statistically // logically** valid. A valid **argument // assumption // opinion // belief // viewpoint // interpretation // explanation**.
validate *v.*	Definition: To confirm or prove.
verify *v.*	Definition: To prove the truth of something.

Practice 16: error correction

Below are ten sentences from real student essays. The sentences are nearly but not quite right (errors are in italics) because the student has used the wrong word, or used the right word but with incorrect form or grammar.

Use the examples and word information above to correct the sentences. Answers are given on p. 131–2.

1 The new company is extremely *innovated*.
2 The National Bureau of Economic Research has been a *great benefit* for the field of economics in recent years.
3 I will look at both the theoretical and *substantial* implications of recent research on the consequences of job insecurity.

4 Lupton (1998) *shows* that the public is interested in health news. However, I will argue that media coverage in this area does not necessarily indicate genuine public interest.

5 Oswald's research *corroborates* the idea that having a job is more significant for happiness than being wealthy.

6 Jack, James and Roger's explanation of the effect of caffeine on performance seems to me the most *possible* because . . .

7 The *viability* of this belief is called into question by recent evidence.

8 Although the survey is *comprehensive*, it fails to look at applications of learning curve theory.

9 Carr (1968) uses the *illustrating* analogy of a poker player to demonstrate his position on business ethics.

10 Importantly, the findings are *consistent to* those of previous studies.

Commenting negatively on a source

The sentences below give you useful vocabulary for introducing, describing and evaluating a source negatively, i.e. in a way that shows you disagree with the source. An important part of developing your argument is to present opposing arguments and to show why they are not as convincing as your own (a process called *rebuttal*). You will often need to give only a brief rebuttal, but you should always do it fairly – don't insult your reader's intelligence by not representing properly the strengths of the opposing arguments. At the end of your rebuttal it is useful to restate how your position differs from that of the opposing arguments

In the example sentences below, words that have similar meanings are grouped together and separated by /. Words that have different meanings but that can be used for the same function and in the same sentence structure are separated by //.

Useful words and phrases

Using neutral verbs to introduce a source and then give a negative comment

- Collins <u>states // claims / maintains // asserts / contends</u> that violence is a product of environmental factors. <u>However</u>, other studies show that . . .
- The report <u>proposes // states / suggests</u> that all students should do an internship. This is <u>not a sensible</u> policy because . . .
- Vellitino <u>examines // considers // covers</u> different concepts of dyslexia <u>but does not</u> identify the synergies between them.

Using negative forms of verbs and negative verbs to comment on a source

- Jones <u>does not consider the fact that // show // establish // demonstrate</u> that the virus has mutated.
- Delaware <u>neglects / overlooks / omits / does not take into account // ignores</u> the fact that . . .
- The study <u>complicates</u> what is in fact a relatively simple phenomenon.
- The report <u>suffers from</u> a lack of detailed analysis.
- The theory of blending inheritance was later <u>disproven / discredited</u> and superseded by the theory of . . .
- The fact there are several digressions <u>detracts from</u> the main argument.
- The diagrams and tables <u>distract</u> (the reader) <u>from</u> the main point of the text.

- The report <u>fails to</u> draw a distinction between children and adults.
- Batiste's assumption that discoveries are always made by developing a theory and then testing it, <u>oversimplifies</u> the process.
- The study <u>manipulates / distorts</u> the findings to fit in with the initial proposition.
- In my view, we can <u>disregard / discount</u> the idea that personality has a major effect on second language acquisition.
- The small sample size should <u>alert</u> us <u>to</u> the fact that the findings may be unreliable.
- Alwald's conclusion seems to <u>conflict with</u> his earlier point that we need new legislation on drug use.
- I suggest that the Copyright Amendment Act is <u>misconceived</u> because . . .

Using negative adjectives and adverbs to comment on a source

- Smith's argument is <u>invalid // flawed // inconsistent // unsound // incoherent // contradictory // problematic // circular // unconvincing</u> because . . .
- Smith's study is <u>inconclusive // limited // questionable // unreliable // unsatisfactory</u> because the sample size is very small.
- Alwald's evidence seems <u>subjective // anecdotal // contradictory // incomplete</u>. He fails to . . .
- The questions in the survey used to gather the data seem somewhat <u>arbitrary // simplistic</u>.
- The report's conclusion is <u>vague</u>. It does not specify . . .
- Patel's model has <u>limited</u> application because it only deals with small-sized businesses.
- The novel's plot is <u>formulaic</u> and has a predictable ending.
- I will show that Peccori <u>wrongly</u> assumes that the correlation between stress and drug use is a causal one.

Using nouns to comment negatively on a source

- The argument business and society are separate is, as I will demonstrate, a <u>fallacy.</u>
- There are both theoretical and practical <u>objections to / problems with</u> the idea of licensing parents. Firstly, . . .
- A <u>serious weakness in / limitation of</u> the argument is that it does not distinguish between volunteers and employees.
- <u>The problem with</u> Kohil's argument <u>is that</u> it does not cover all possible situations.
- One <u>flaw</u> in the study is that it is <u>biased</u> towards Western cultures.
- The research team seem <u>to show a disregard for</u> proper contamination control.
- Tse <u>offers no explanation</u> as to why left-handedness might be caused by complications at birth.
- The report suffers from <u>a lack of / absence of</u> detailed analysis.
- A <u>conspicuous / noticeable omission</u> is that the analysis does not include children.
- There are several <u>digressions</u> that detract from the main argument.
- The many anecdotes are <u>a distraction</u> from the main point of the text.
- The authors <u>make no attempt to</u> present or evaluate the counterarguments.

Describing specific flaws in the logic of an argument

- The absence of women in the study means that his conclusions are an <u>overgeneralization</u>.

- Saying that an opt-out system is good because it ensures organs are donated unless specified otherwise, is a <u>circular</u> argument.
- The minister offered the <u>non sequitur</u> that because identity theft is increasing, we should introduce identity cards.
- Ormazabal (2003) argues that there is a <u>contradiction</u> in Keynes' definition of income.
- The report concludes with the <u>tautological statement / tautology</u> that the economy will either improve or will not.
- Buchanan offered the <u>truism</u> that to achieve good public health, all sections of the community need adequate housing.
- The argument that the UK economy will be stronger if we leave the EU is <u>irrational / illogical</u> because . . .

Stating that an argument is not supported by other research

- Lock's idea is <u>not supported by / not corroborated by // contradictory to // undermined by</u> other research.
- This claim is <u>called into question by / conflicts with / is contradicted by / is inconsistent with</u> later studies.
- <u>The problem with</u> Kohil's argument <u>is that it is not supported by any other evidence</u>.

Stating how research or an argument could have been better

- The report <u>would have been more convincing // persuasive // effective if</u> it had used more recent data.

Conceding up to a point and then disagreeing

- Translators are necessary <u>but</u> can't always convey fully the author's meaning.
- <u>Although</u> translators are necessary, <u>I have shown that</u> they can't always convey the author's exact meaning.
- <u>Notwithstanding the fact that / Despite the fact that</u> translators are essential, they often can't convey . . .
- Translators are essential. <u>Nonetheless, / Nevertheless, / However,</u> I have shown that they cannot fully convey . . .
- <u>While I don't agree with</u> Dawkins that religious education is indoctrination, <u>I do think that</u> he <u>has a valid point when</u> he says . . .
- <u>Although I think it is going too far to say that</u> unions are redundant, <u>we should be willing to concede / accept / acknowledge that</u> . . .
- <u>I disagree with</u> Collins <u>on the extent to which</u> businesses should be ethical <u>but I do agree with</u> his basic proposition.

Stating clearly that you disagree

- I <u>refute / contest // reject // rebut</u> Lei's <u>idea // claim // argument</u> and <u>offer the alternative suggestion that</u> . . .
- I <u>counter</u> Wolf's hypothesis with the suggestion that businesses and society are interdependent.

- I <u>don't agree / disagree (with the view) that</u> grammar should be taught explicitly and have shown that . . .
- <u>My rebuttal</u> to the argument for 'human' global warming <u>is based on the fact that</u> temperature variations are . . .
- <u>In my view the main flaw in // problem with // limitation of</u> Bernhard's hypothesis <u>is that</u> it is too restrictive. <u>I therefore offer an alternative view, which is that</u> . . .
- <u>I would argue that the opposite is probably / likely to be the case</u> because . . .

Information on some of these words

anecdotal *adj.*	Definition: Information that comes from casual observation or from only one or two sources, and which is, therefore, not a reliable basis from which to make generalisations or draw conclusions.
arbitrary *adj.*	Definition: Actions or decisions that are based on unjustified, random premises and assumptions.
bias *n.*	Definition: The treatment of something in an unequal / partial manner.
circular *adj.*	Definition: A logical fallacy whereby an argument is 'empty' because the conclusion is merely a restatement of the premise(s) and so assumes as true what it is trying to prove. For example: 'Wearing a helmet when cycling is advisable because it makes sense to do so.'
conspicuous *adj.*	Definition: Clearly visible, noticeable. Often (but not always) used in a negative context. For example: A conspicuous flaw // deficiency // absence.
contest *n./v.*	Definition: *v.* – To argue against a statement. Similar to *refute* and *rebut*. Common phrases: To contest the **claim // suggestion // accusation // idea // theory**
contradiction *n.* **contradict** *v.* **contradictory** *adj.*	Definition: *n.* – In argument, such that two or more statements cannot both/all be true.
detract *v.* **detraction** *n.*	Definition: *v.* – To reduce the value or worth of something or to make it seem less impressive. For example: 'The diagrams detract from the main point because they are not directly related to it.' Commonly confused: *detract* and *distract* (see below).
digress *v.* **digression** *n.*	Definition: *v.* – To move away from the main topic / issue.

discount *v./n.*   Definition: *v.* – To disregard or leave out something because it lacks validity and/or importance.
n. – A deduction from the original price.

discredit *v.*   Definition: (1) In academic study, to cause evidence or ideas to seem unreliable or false.
(2) To damage someone's reputation in some way.
Common phrases: To discredit an **argument // idea // theory // research**.

distort *v.*
distortion *n.*   Definition: *v.* – To give a misleading or false impression, or to misrepresent.
Common phrases: To distort (the) **facts // evidence // findings // results // truth // understanding // reality**.

distract *v.*
distraction *n.*   Definition: *v.* – To take attention, concentration or focus away from something else.
Common phrases: X distracts Y from the **main aim / goal / purpose / objective**.
Commonly confused: *distract* and *detract*.
These two words have different meanings; see above for *detract*.

fallacy *n.*
fallacious *adj.*   Definition: *n.* – A commonly held idea or belief that is false.
In formal logic, a fallacy is any form of incorrect reasoning that leads to an invalid argument.
Examples of logical fallacies are non sequiturs (see below) and false analogies or comparisons.

flaw *n.*
flawed *adj.*   Definition: *n.* – A defect, shortcoming or underlying weakness.

formulaic *adj.*   Definition: Not original or interesting because it uses a standard and much-used format.

incoherent *adj.*   Definition: Not logical and poorly structured.

inconclusive *adj.*   Definition: Not producing a definite result or conclusion.
Common phrases: To **be // remain // prove** inconclusive.

inconsistent *adj.*   Definition: (1) Unstable, changing in some way, or acting in a different way than previously.
(2) Contradictory.

invalid *adj.*
invalidity *n.*   Definition: *adj.* – (1) In logic, an invalid argument is one that contains flawed reasoning, i.e. where the conclusion does not necessarily follow from the premises. A non sequitur is an example of an invalid argument (see below).
(2) Not legally recognised.

manipulate *v.*

Definition: (1) To alter or present information in a way that is purposely misleading.
(2) To move, handle or control, usually by using the hands.
(3) To influence and/or control another person.

misconceive *v.*
misconception *n.*

Definition: *v.* – (1) To plan or judge something poorly or incorrectly.
(2) To misunderstand.
n. – An incorrect belief or opinion.

non sequitur *n.*

Definition: A statement that does not follow logically from the one before, or when a conclusion is based on insufficient, incorrect or irrelevant reasoning. In formal logic, a non sequitur is when a conclusion does not follow from its premise(s).
For example: All bikes have wheels. This car has wheels, therefore this car is a bike.

objection *n.*
object *v./n.*

Definition: *n.* – A reason for disagreeing with or disapproving of something.
Common phrases: A **chief / main /primary /principal // fundamental // formal** objection.

omission *n.*
omit *v.*

Definition: *n.* – Something left out or a failure to do something.

overgeneralise *v.*
overgeneralisation *n.*

Definition: *v.* – To make a generalisation (i.e. to apply a specific case to a wider range of situations) that is too broad to be justified. For example: 'People are healthier now than they were twenty years ago.'

oversimplify *v.*
oversimplification *n.*

Definition: *v.* – To explain something (usually a cause and effect process) so that it seems simpler than it actually is.
For example: 'Sugar makes you fat.'
Commonly confused: *overgeneralise* and *oversimplify*.
These words are often confused. As shown in the definitions here, an overgeneralisation is a statement that is incorrect because it is <u>applied</u> too broadly, not because it oversimplifies a situation or process.
Common phrases: *v.* – To **slightly // greatly** oversimplify.
n. – A **slight // gross** oversimplification.

questionable *adj.*

Definition: (1) Open to doubt or challenge regarding quality, accuracy or truth.
(2) Of someone's character, not very honest or respectable.

rebut *v.*
rebuttal *n.*

Definition: *v.* – To argue against a statement. Similar to *contest* and *refute* but less commonly used.

refute *n.*

Definition: To oppose a statement and, importantly, to try to prove that the statement is false. Similar to *contest* and *rebut*.

Common phrases: To refute the **claim // suggestion // accusation // idea // theory** that...

reject *v./n.*

Definition: To not accept.
Commonly confused: *reject, refute* and *deny.*
Reject has the more general meaning.
To refute is a more formal word used only in the context of argument and ideas. It differs from both *reject* and *deny* because *refute* must include giving reasons for not accepting a statement.
To deny often means to reject an accusation or the truth of something, and is not usually appropriate in an academic context.

simplistic *adj.*

Definition: (Much) simpler than is actually the case and therefore misleading.
Common phrases: A simplistic **approach // argument // assumption // description // explanation // view.**

subjective *adj.*

Definition: Based on your feelings and beliefs rather than evidence or fact. Opposite of *objective.*

tautology *n.*
tautological *adj.*

Definition: *n.* – A sentence or phrase that merely repeats itself. Tautologies are common in everyday language.
For example: 'A free gift', 'joined together', 'in close proximity'.

truism *n.*

Definition: An obviously true and uninteresting statement that is therefore not worth making.
Commonly confused: *truism* and *axiom.*
These words can be interchanged, but an axiom can also refer to a statement that is actually useful because it establishes a basic premise or principle from which to analyse an argument. *Axiom* is often used in mathematics and philosophy and the adjective *axiomatic* is used in many disciplines.
For example: 'It's axiomatic to say that economic growth relies on production.'

undermine *v.*

Definition: To cause something to become less confident, successful or powerful.
Common phrases: To undermine **credibility // validity // trust // support // confidence // value // stability // democracy.**
To undermine a/an **principle // argument // belief // idea // theory.**

vague *adj.*

Definition: Imprecise, indefinite or unclear.
Commonly confused: *vague* and *ambiguous.*
These words have different meanings. Something is ambiguous if it has more than one possible meaning and so may be interpreted differently in different contexts.

Practice 17: error correction

Below are ten sentences from real student essays. The sentences are nearly but not quite right (errors are in italics) because the student has used the wrong word, or used the right word but with incorrect form or grammar. Use the examples and word information above to correct the sentences.

Answers are given on p. 132.

1 To state that cancer is caused by obesity is an *overgeneralisation*.
2 The study *alleged* that mass media can be used to educate children but this was not borne out by the evidence.
3 The conclusion is contradicted *with* the data given earlier in the paper.
4 Tanen (2000) *established* that visual imprinting occurs in infancy. However, this was shown to be incorrect by later studies.
5 Bijal (2002) *fails to neglect* the fact that in most urban areas rich and poor sometimes live in close proximity.
6 Smith's study is *limiting* because the sample size is extremely small.
7 The experiment was conducted according to a *formulaic* method in order to ensure reliability.
8 The arguments in Bazer's article have a strong *bias* of Eurocentric.
9 Hooper's theory of the origin of the HIV virus is *suffering from* lack of evidence
10 The theory was *given discredit* in 2001, when it was shown that there was no evidence to support it.

Practice 18: evaluating a source negatively

Below is part of the student's critical analysis of the Albert Carr article from p. 22. Use this informal analysis to write a more formal essay paragraph that gives some negative comments about the article.

An example essay paragraph is given in the answer section on p. 132.

Extract from the student's informal critical analysis of the Carr article

His style is quite persuasive – I instinctively feel he is partly right – but he is very cynical and oversimplifies. He gives no evidence for his views and doesn't try to be objective or look at opposing evidence. His argument isn't very well-ordered as it is continuous opinion rather than a developed argument. I agree with Carr that some people feel they do need to lie in business but not that this is always the case or that business ethics are totally separate from social norms – not true nowadays?

Techniques for re-expressing sources

Five useful techniques

Remember that when you paraphrase or summarise, it is not enough simply to replace individual words one by one from the source with your own words; doing this results in a paraphrase that is too similar to the original, mainly because it will have the same sentence pattern. To avoid this trap, make sure that you fully understand the text or text section before you start writing and that you can restate it in your own independent way.

It is useful to be aware of some basic ways of using vocabulary and grammar to help you use your own words and sentence structures to rewrite your source material. Five useful techniques are:

- using a different word that has the same meaning as the original one (a synonym);
- changing the form of a word;
- changing the tense of a verb;
- changing the structure of the sentence;
- changing the order of the information.

Below is the text extract we used in section A5, followed by an acceptable paraphrase.

Source extract

> So far there is no clear evidence from health studies of a relation between mobile phone use and mortality or morbidity. Indeed, tantalising findings in humans include a speeding up of reaction time during exposure, particularly during behavioural tasks calling for attention and electrical brain activity changes during cognitive processes. It is not clear, however, whether these findings have any positive implications for health.
>
> Adapted from: Maier, M., Blakemore, C. and Koivisto, M. (2000) 'The health hazards of mobile phones' *British Medical Journal*, 320(7245), pp. 1288–1289.

Acceptable paraphrase

Studies point to interesting results suggesting that mobile phone users experience quicker reaction times to some tasks which require both changes in electrical brain activity and concentration (Maier et al. 2000). Although it has not been shown that that this effect represents an actual benefit to health, there has equally been no hard data from any disease studies to suggest that mobile phones actually damage health in any way (ibid.).

ibid. = from the same place/source as previously mentioned.

Below is a list giving examples of showing how the five techniques were used in the paraphrase of the article extract.

- **Using synonyms**
  'tantalising findings' changed to 'interesting results'
  'mortality and morbidity' changed to 'disease studies'
  'clear evidence' changed to 'hard data'
- **Changing the word form**
  'mobile phone use' (noun) changed to 'using' (verb)
- **Changing the tense, mood or voice of the verb**
  'there is no clear evidence of' (present simple) changed to 'there has been no hard data' (present perfect passive)
- **Changing the order of the information**
  In his paraphrase, the student has reversed the order of the two main points given in the source extract.
- **Changing the structure of the sentence**
  The student has put two points together in his last sentence and has used a sentence structure with *although* that was not in the original extract.

Practice 19: increase your awareness of techniques for paraphrasing

Read the source extract and paraphrase below. Look at whether and/or how the student has used the five techniques described above in their paraphrase. Answers are given on p. 133.
You may also like to look again at p. 38 (*Source Extract 2* and *Essay extract 2*) showing how the student used their paraphrase of this extract in their essay.

Source extract
. . .there is indeed considerable overlap between ethics and the law. In fact, the law is essentially and institutionalisation or codification of ethics into specific social rules, regulations, and proscriptions. Nevertheless, the two are not equivalent. . . .The law might be said to be a definition of the minimum acceptable standards of behaviour. However, many morally contestable issues, whether in business of elsewhere, are not explicitly covered by the law. . . . In one sense then, business ethics can be said to begin where the law ends. Business ethics is primarily concerned with those issues not covered by the law, or where there is no definite consensus on whether something is right or wrong.

Extracts from: Crane, A. and Matten, D. (2010) *Business Ethics.* pp. 5 and 7.

Student paraphrase
It is important to emphasise here that business ethics is not synonymous with legality. Business ethics is mainly concerned with areas of conduct that are *not* specifically covered by law and that are therefore open to different interpretations, a fact that means a particular behaviour may be legal, albeit viewed as unethical (Crane and Matten 2010). There is some overlap between law and ethics, but legislation usually only regulates the lowest level of acceptable behaviour (ibid.).

Practice 20: write a paraphrase

Read the text extract below a couple to times and make notes. When you are sure that you understand the extract properly and can put it into your own words and style, use the five techniques described in this section to help you write a paraphrase of the extract. An example paraphrase is given on p. 133.

Source extract

Every day, in every industrialised country of the world, journalists and politicians give out a conscious and unconscious message. It is that better economic performance means more happiness for a nation. This idea is rarely questioned. We feel we would be more cheery if our boss raised our pay, and assume that countries must be roughly the same. The results in this paper suggest that, in a developed nation, economic progress buys only a small amount of extra happiness.

Extract from: Oswald, A.J. (1997) 'Happiness and economic performance'
The Economic Journal, 107, No. 445 pp. 1815–1831.

Vocabulary and writing style

As explained in the introduction to Part B, you need to use a fairly formal style in your academic writing that will enable you to express complex ideas precisely. Remember, however, that you also need to write in a way that is clear and to the point and not overly complicated or formal. Below are four key points that will help you use formal vocabulary and write in a clear and precise manner.

1 Use nouns

Read the two paraphrases below. Both paraphrases give the same correct information (the results of the Cote and Morgan experiment) but in different writing styles.

Paraphrase 1

Cote and Morgan did an experiment, and they showed that people make or pretend to make themselves feel happier more often than they try to hide feeling unhappy or angry. Another important thing they found out was that the way you hide or alter your feelings can have a big effect on how happy you are with your job, and whether or not you think you want to leave it. However, they didn't find any evidence that people are affected the other way round, that how you feel about your job and leaving it affects how much you hide or change your emotions.

Paraphrase 2

Cote and Morgan's data showed that the amplification of pleasant emotions happened more frequently than the suppression of unpleasant ones. Importantly, they also found a strong correlation between emotion regulation and job satisfaction and intention to quit. However, there was no strong evidence to suggest the reverse correlation, namely, that job satisfaction and intention to quit influence emotional regulation.

Commentary on the paraphrases

Paraphrase 1 is written in a fairly informal style which uses lots of subject and verb phrases (e.g. *people make, they try to hide, the way you hide, if you think, how you feel*). You may quite like this style, and there is nothing grammatically incorrect about it; however, the constant use of *they/you* is too personal and also distracts the reader from the information being discussed.

Paraphrase 2 is written in a more formal style that tends to use nouns (*amplification, emotions, suppression, correlation, job satisfaction, intention, emotional regulation*) rather than subject/verb phrases. This gives more emphasis to the information, and makes the extract more clear, concise and powerful. A good technique is to start a sentence or phrase with the key idea in the form of a noun.

One word of caution – although using nouns is good, don't use too many abstract nouns (ones that end in *-tion, -ism, -ness, -nce, -ity*) in one sentence, as this may make it clumsy and unclear. In these cases it may be better to use the verb/adjective form instead.

For example:

The <u>organisation</u> of the <u>compilation</u> of the legislation was poor. ✗
The <u>compilation</u> of the legislation <u>was</u> poorly <u>organised</u>. ✔

2 Use one-word verbs

Avoid using two-word verb such as *make up, get round, go up, help out* and *find out.* This type of verb is too informal and often imprecise. Use a more formal, one-word equivalent such as *compensate, avoid, increase, assist, discover.* Phrases which use the verbs *get* and *go* (e.g. 'It's getting worse' / 'it goes round in circles') are usually too informal for academic writing.

3 Be clear and to the point

Writing in a formal style and discussing complex ideas does *not* mean that you have to use as many 'long words' as possible, and academic articles that do so are probably poorly written. Aim to convey complex ideas with brevity and avoid using words that are overly-complicated or that merely repeat the previous word.

For example:

This essay will commence with ✗/ start with ✔
The experiment endeavours to ✗ / tries to ✔
The tower was fabricated in ✗ / built in ✔
We utilised ✗ / used ✔ three different methods
absolutely essential ✗ – essential ✔
past history ✗ – history ✔
conclusive proof ✗ – proof ✔
revert back to ✗– revert to ✔
hard evidence ✗ – evidence ✔
close proximity ✗ – proximity ✔
different varieties ✗ – varieties ✔
join together ✗ – join ✔
or, alternatively ✗ – alternatively ✔
true facts ✗ – facts ✔

4. Avoid informal words and phrases

In paraphrase 1 above, the words *big* and *thing* were used. Such words are too informal and imprecise for academic writing. Table 3 lists some more words and phrases that students sometimes use in their essays but which are too informal for academic writing; do not use them.

Table 3   Words and phrases that are too informal for academic writing

Imprecise, incomplete or lazy	Too emotional, subjective or informal	Redundant phrases	Sayings or clichés
etc.	terrible	basically	in a nutshell
and so on	incredible	it all comes down to	last but not least
and so forth	awful	at the end of the day	to put it mildly
thing	pretty (meaning 'very')	after all	to name but a few
stuff	obvious	the thing is	no-one is perfect
a bit	really and truly	along the way	
sort of	surely	when it comes down to it	
	everyone knows that	anyway	
	it's unfair that		
	it's a great way of		
	it is so hard		
	it is such hard work		
	it is all too much		
	it's just not on		

Practice 21: error correction

Below are real student sentences that contain informal words or phrases. Correct or rewrite these sentences. Suggested answers are on pp. 133–134.

1 Globalisation is *very bad for* the planet.
2 Some companies behave unethically *and this kind of thing must stop.*
3 The issue will be *sorted* by the government.
4 *Basically,* there is no evidence that mobile phone use damages health.
5 *It all comes down to whether or not you can* regulate your emotions.
6 The dangers of cloning are *mind-boggling.*
7 *The point is,* companies need to pay more attention to business ethics.
8 Children who use drugs are often *left out in the dark.*
9 *The way this is going* there will not be enough resources.
10 They were *bewildered* by the results.
11 Organ transplantation is *just* not effective.
12 Patients should not be treated *at all* like this.
13 We should *leave them alone.*
14 It will not help us *anyway.*
15 *It's a whole different ball game.*

16 The situation *can't go on like this*.
17 Globalisation can only lead to *the downfall of mankind*.
18 There are different kinds of businesses, private, public, non-profit making *etc*.
19 It's a *pretty big* problem.
20 The most important *thing to do* is to reduce carbon emissions.

Practice 22: using a formal style

The paraphrase below is written in a style that is too informal. Rewrite it in a more formal style, replacing the subject/verb phrases with nouns where possible and appropriate. A suggested answer is given on p. 134.

Paraphrase written in an informal style

Cote and Morgan showed that as they thought would happen, if you keep a tight lid on bad feelings, you will be pretty unhappy with your job and so you'll be more likely to think about leaving it. Their research results also say that basically, if you increase your happy emotions, you'll feel loads better about your job because you'll get on better at your place of work, and on top of this you'll get better responses from your workmates and customers.

Checking and correcting your work

Introduction to Part C: key points for checking your work

Making significant changes to your essay is all part of the rewriting, checking and polishing process. As well as making changes in structure and content, you also need to check your work for mistakes with individual words, grammar and punctuation. You do need to check and correct these smaller errors, because accuracy in grammar, vocabulary and punctuation is highly valued in academic work and greatly increases the credibility of your work. Even though you might only make mistakes on one or two grammatical points, making these repeatedly will detract from your writing. Many students would get much higher marks for their work if they checked it carefully, not once but at least three times. Professional writers will often re-read and amend their work at least seven or eight times.

Part C sections

Part C focuses on common grammatical mistakes students make when they are using and commenting on sources in their essays.

Part C gives you:

- sentences containing common student errors with in-essay referencing for you to correct;
- a brief explanation of grammatical points that are common sources of student error;
- real student sentences containing other common error types for you to correct.

Part A and Part B of *How to Use your Reading in your Essays* have taken you through the process of using sources in your writing and have given you useful vocabulary for doing so. Part C completes this process by giving you information to help you improve your grammatical accuracy when using sources, raising your awareness of common error types and giving you practice in spotting and correcting them so that you can avoid making them in your own work.

The explanations of grammatical points in section C2 are intended as a brief revision and clarification on problem areas, and so you may need to do some further work of your own on particular points. For this reason the main grammatical terms are explained for each point covered and Appendix 6 on page 154 gives you a brief explanation of different word classes. You will probably find some sections in Part C more useful than others, so use them in any order, as and when you need.

Tips for checking your work

- Make sure you leave plenty of time for checking and correcting your work. Re-reading and amending your assignment several times is a key part of the writing process, not something that should be left to the last minute.

- Once you have finished writing your essay, put it away for at least a few hours or overnight if you can – the longer the better.

- Try printing your essay out and checking this paper version rather than checking your work on screen. Reading a paper version may help you to see your essay in a fresh and more objective way, almost as someone else's work, and you will spot mistakes more easily. Remember that you must try to see what you have actually written, rather than what you *think* you have written.

- Reading a paper version of your work slowly out loud is an effective way of hearing mistakes you might not detect just by reading your work through in your mind. (You can also try recording yourself reading out your work and then playing the recording back.) Getting someone else to read out your work to you will ensure that you hear what you have actually put on the page.

- When you have corrected the mistakes you find, print out and read out your essay again. Remember that the grammar and spell check on your computer will only detect a very limited range of mistakes, and that they are not a substitute for your own careful checking and correcting.

- The more you practise checking and correcting your writing, the better you will become at doing it. Being able to edit your work is an important skill, not just for university study but also for your future career. Some students do not realise how important it is to check their CV and job application – you should re-read your CV at least five or six times before sending it off. A CV sent to an employer containing more than couple of minor mistakes will often be put straight into the bin.

Common mistakes with in-essay references

This section contains student errors relating to different aspects of in-essay referencing (the errors are not highlighted). Identify the mistake or mistakes in each sentence and correct them. Answers and comments are given on pages 134–135.

Mistakes when referring to the source or author

Below are student sentences that contain mistakes in the way that the student has referred to the source or author in their essay.

Practice 23: error correction

1 According to (Dr Reynolds 2000) there is no strong evidence of long-term damage to health.
2 According to Dr Padash 2000 there is no strong evidence of long-term damage to health.
3 George Marchais (1984) discusses three main factors.
4 Locke (97) suggests that we need more evidence.
5 'Global warming is a factual truth' (Greenpeace article).
6 The website has drawn attention to the fact that more research needs to be done.
7 A strong economy relies on moderate taxation methods (Sloman, Economics 3rd Edition).
8 These factors can be seen in the article titled 'Biometric data of the future'.
9 'Locke and Himenez' show that early pre-school learning improves children's ability to process information.
10 Smoking and related illness causes over 500,000 deaths annually in the UK.
11 **Folour and Skipton** (1991) found a strong correlation between amount of exposure to sunlight and depression.
12 Smith's article entitled location and personal identity, demonstrates how closely the two are related.

Mistakes when using the words *according to, quote, cite* or *source.*

When you quote or paraphrase a source, you should not use the words *quote* or *cite* unless you are stating that one author has cited or quoted another. You should not talk about the process you went through of researching and reading sources for your essay unless you are specifically asked to do so.

Practice 24: error correction

1 According to me, the issue of global warming is not as serious as the media portrays.
2 Kerlinger (1969) quotes that: '*Science* is a misused and misunderstood word' (p. 1127).
3 From the published book written by Jones (2002) we can see that governments need to address this issue urgently.
4 As Collins (1994) cites, 'good ethics is synonymous with good management' (p. 2).
5 These factors are discussed in the source 'Dying to be thin'.
6 After researching many sources and reading eight articles over the last two weeks, I have found that the issue of global warming is controversial.

Mistakes with sentence grammar

Points to note are:

- if you use the author or article as the subject of your sentence, you should not also use words such as *it* or *they / their research*;
- if you use the structure *As* X *states / shows / demonstrates…* do not use *that* after the verb.

Practice 25: error correction

1 Cote and Morgan (2002) their research showed that emotion regulation affects job satisfaction.
2 Coates and Bailey (1995) their study examined three main aspects of mental health.
3 According to the *New Scientist* (8/1/2005), it states that people are still not aware of the effects the use of mobile phones can have.
4 As Crème and Lea (1997) stated, that the gap between academic and personal writing is not as far apart as we assume.
5 According to Smith (2000) states that the problem is widespread.

Mistakes with grammar and punctuation when using quotations

(See also p. 36 for a relevant correction practice exercise.)

Practice 26: error correction

1 In addition to this, 'effects on memory and attention and how microwaves alter electrical activity on the brain' will also be studied". (*New Scientist* (2005)))
2 Knowles (1998) 'It has to be stated that groups work more efficiently' (p. 64).
3 Jones 2006 'importance of understanding the causes of mental ill health' (p. 12).

Ten grammatical areas that cause problems

Below are brief explanations of ten points that are common sources of error in student writing. The information on each point is followed by a few student sentences containing typical errors for you to correct (the errors are not highlighted). Answers and comments on the practice exercises are on pages 135–9.

1 *Important* or *importance*?

As stated in Part B, you need to make sure that you use the correct form of a word. Definitions and examples of the basic word forms are given below. Your dictionary will also give you the different forms of a word. See also Appendix 6, p. 154 for a brief explanation of word class.

noun – a place, person or thing.
For example: an article, a book, an essay title, research.

Many nouns used in academic writing are abstract (things you can't actually touch or see). For example, an issue, a theory, a problem, a debate, an argument, a discussion, an assumption, an increase, research, information, a conclusion, importance, relevance, consideration.

adjective – describes a noun.
For example: a *long* article, *rigorous* research, a *controversial* debate, a *flawed* assumption, a *clear* conclusion, a *relevant* model, a *problematic* issue, *conclusive* results, a *considerable* amount of research.

verb – an action or state.
For example: to be, to argue, to show, to increase, to debate, to discuss, to theorise, to problematise, to conclude, to imply, to consider.

adverb – usually describes a verb (adverbs can also describe an adjective or another adverb) and often ends in –ly.
For example: It is *arguably* the most important issue. It *conclusively* shows that the drugs are ineffective. This view has been *positively* demonstrated. The rate has increased *considerably*.

Note that different forms of a word sometimes have different meanings. For example, *a conclusion* means 'the end of something'. However, *conclusive* and *conclusively* mean 'definite' or 'definitely'.

Practice 27: error correction

1 Knowles (2000) difference between the theory and practice of primary education.
2 The population rose by three percentage a year.
3 Countries are making changes to suit tourisms.
4 The process has advantageous.
5 The process continuous to the final stage.
6 This has made a great contributing to society.
7 The article clear states that more research needs to be conducted.
8 Some people have strong religion believes.
9 A vital factor in counselling is trust and confident.
10 Conclusively, this essay has shown that this question needs further investigation.
11 The main negative factors in organ transplantation are the expense of the operation, the length of waiting time and risking your health.
12 There is still a potentially market.

2 Have or has?

Subject and verb agreement for the third person singular

In your essays you will often need to use the third person singular subject *he, she, it*, or equivalents such as *Smith / the software / the experiment / the research / this essay*.

With the **third person singular**, regular verbs in the present tense use **verb +s**. The verb *'to be'* uses *is / has been / was*, and the verb *'to have'* uses *has / has had / had*. (See Table 4.) For example:

> The experiment show<u>s</u> that / The experiment <u>is</u> flawed / This experiment <u>has</u> credibility.

Having an *s* at the end of a verb for a singular subject can seem confusing, because an *s* is usually associated with plurals, but you do need to make sure that you follow the rules, as shown below.

Table 4   The third person singular verb form

Third person singular subject +	Verb
he / she / it / Smith / the book / the article / the experiment / the research team / the author / the theory / the issue / the debate / the data	Present tense regular verbs: *show<u>s</u> / report<u>s</u> / involve<u>s</u> / increase<u>s</u> / conclude<u>s</u>*
	To be: *i<u>s</u> / wa<u>s</u> / ha<u>s</u> been*
	To have: *ha<u>s</u> / had / ha<u>s</u> had*

Subject and verb agreement for plural subjects

For **plural subjects**, the grammatical rule is that the *s* is put with the subject, not the verb.

Table 5 The plural subject verb form		
Plural subjects: we/they/you +	*Verb*	
The books / the authors / the issues / the results / the research projects	Present tense regular verbs: *show / report / involve / increase / conclude*	
	To be: *are / were / have been* To have: *have / had / have had*	

Uncountable nouns

These are nouns that cannot be used on their own as a plural and are **only used in the third person singular**. Some uncountable nouns are used frequently in academic writing. For example:

> The research shows that… / The equipment is expensive. / Progress has been made. / The information was useful. There is evidence to suggest that… .

Examples of uncountable nouns include words that refer to academic disciplines, for example, *genetics, mathematics* and *linguistics.* Note that although these words end in an *s* they are uncountable and used only as a singular subject.

Other uncountable nouns commonly used in academic writing are *research / equipment / information / technology / energy / evidence / proof,* and most abstract nouns such as *importance / knowledge / intelligence / motivation / education / satisfaction / happiness.*

Countable nouns

Countable nouns can be used as a singular subject (verb + s) or as a plural subject. For example:

> The researcher has shown that AND The researchers have shown that / The research project involves AND The research projects involve.

Common countable nouns used in academic writing include *researcher / project / statistics / study / experiment / theory / finding / result / essay.*

Subject and verb agreement of some common phrases

- **Common phrases that use the third person singular (verb + s)**
  It is either the first or the second solution that has contaminated the slides.
  Neither Wolf nor Carr feels that businesses should concern themselves with ethics.
  Everyone / anyone / someone /no one understands that . . .
  Another problem is . . .
  The (total) number of cases is not significant.
  The total of 120 was higher than expected.
  The average age is . . .
  A large / small / significant amount of work has been done on this topic.

- **Common phrases that use a plural form**
  There are <u>many</u> projects / There are <u>few</u> studies.
  <u>Other</u> issue<u>s</u> <u>include</u> the expense and the health risks.
  <u>A</u> (large / small / significant) <u>number of</u> patient<u>s</u> <u>have</u> recovered.

- **Common phrases that can use the third person singular *or* plural subject**
  If the first noun in the sentence is a fraction, percentage or proportion, the verb
  should agree with the noun <u>closest</u> to it. If the closest noun is singular or
  uncountable, the verb form is singular (verb +s). If the closest noun is plural, the
  verb form should be plural (no s). For example:

  > The majority / a minority / 60% / two thirds /a quarter of the <u>population</u> <u>is</u> in
  > agreement on the issue.
  > The majority / a minority /60% / two thirds /a quarter of the respondent<u>s</u> <u>are</u>
  > in agreement on the issue.

Practice 28: error correction

1 The number of tourists have increased.
2 Smith et al. (2000) reports that this level of violence is harmful.
3 Recent research also show that the drugs are effective.
4 The stress response help the body to react.
5 Malicious software such as worms have been increasingly used.
6 The two types differs in the way they can be treated.
7 A research company have recently produced a new report.
8 Kline imply that ethics is not important.
9 The use of mobile phones have long term effects.
10 Many research are carried out in laboratories.
11 A large amount of water are reabsorbed in the colon.
12 One of the main differences are the weight.
13 Many information can be collected via the questionnaires.

3. Sentence and clause structure

Missing verbs

Don't forget that all full sentences must contain at least one verb.

Practice 29: error correction

1 For example, the risk to the health of the patients.
2 Firstly, the positive aspects of drug therapy.
3 An increasing number of people difficult to get a job.
4 Guideline daily amounts on food labels an alternative to the traffic light system of labelling.
5 The majority of drug users aged between eighteen and thirty.

Missing clauses

A clause is a word group that has at least a subject and something that comes after it, usually a verb. Some clauses can stand alone as a sentence and are called dependent clauses.

> For example: 'Svennson and Wood claim that businesses and society are interconnected.'

Other clauses (such as those beginning with *although, though, even though, because, since, if, unless, when, whether, while, whereas, until, which, that* or *who*) cannot stand alone and must be followed by a second clause to form a complete sentence. These are called dependent clauses.

> For example: 'Whereas Wolf claims that businesses should only be concerned with making a profit, . . .'

Practice 30: error correction

1 Although there are several advantages.
2 Our data, which shows a direct correlation between lack of light and depression.
3 As they have found that it contains several inconsistencies.
4 As well as giving out benefits to families in poverty.
5 Owing to fears about levels of media attention.
6 Even though the participants suffered mild side-effects.

Missing *that*

Some reporting verbs usually need to be followed by *that* + clause. These include *accept, agree, argue, claim, conclude, propose, recommend, show, state* and *suggest*.
Note that the verbs *discuss* and *debate* are **not** followed by *that*.

Practice 31: error correction

1 Dorkin argues if people want to eliminate poverty, taxes must be increased.
2 Herschel points out the theory of relativity is difficult to understand fully.
3 Donne states the experiment was a success in terms of raising further questions for study.
4 Lockheart demonstrates after children have played violent computer games, their behaviour is more aggressive.
5 The study suggests when people are highly dependent on each other, they tend to be more altruistic.
6 Hanson claims the way we interpret the world around us depends on our linguistic and cultural background.

Too many clauses in one sentence

A sentence that has four or more clauses might be difficult for your reader to follow (for example, sentence 1 in practice exercise 32 below has four clauses) so avoid such sentence structures wherever possible.

Run-on sentences and comma splices

A run-on sentence is where independent clauses (clauses that can stand alone as a sentence) are run together without adequate use of a linking word or punctuation.

> For example: 'We conducted the experiment <u>twice we found</u> no long-term effects.' ✗
> 'We conducted the experiment twice and found no long-term <u>effects however further</u> testing is needed before the drug can be marketed safely.' ✗

Note that separating such clauses using only a comma is also incorrect (a mistake called a comma splice).

> For example: 'We conducted the experiment <u>twice, we</u> found no long-term effects.' ✗
> 'We conducted the experiment twice and found no long-term <u>effects, however</u> further testing is needed before the drug can be marketed safely.' ✗

To correct a run-on sentence or comma splice you can add an appropriate co-ordinating word (e.g. *and / but / yet / or / so / for / nor*).

> For example: We conducted the experiment <u>twice and we</u> found no long-term effects.' ✔

With more complex structures you will probably need to split the clauses into two sentences.

> For example: We conducted the experiment twice and found not long-term <u>effects. However,</u> further testing is needed before the drug can be marketed safely.' ✔

Practice 32: error correction

1 Cote and Morgan have shown that emotion regulation influences job satisfaction and that amplifying positive emotions increases positive interaction with both colleagues and customers but that there is not an opposite correlation, that is, that job satisfaction affects emotion regulation.

2 The business decisions managers take can have significant implications, most managers do not have training in business ethics.

3 The worldwide web is a constantly developing technology, it has many advantages for society.

4 Lupton (1998) claims that the public is interested in health news, however, I will argue that media coverage does not indicate genuine public interest.

5 Wolf (2008) argues that business should not concern itself with social consequences, on the other hand, Svensson and Wood claim that business and society are co-dependent.

4 In, at or on?

Prepositions describe the relationship, in either time or space, between two things. Examples of prepositions are *in* / *at* / *on* / *over* / *for* / *through* / *between* and *during*.

It is important to use the correct preposition, as they all describe different relationships. For example:

Research <u>on</u> nuclear physics
Research <u>by</u> Jones
Research <u>for</u> the government
Research <u>under</u> Dr Patel
Research <u>at</u> the hospital

Some words only ever use one specific preposition; your dictionary should tell you which preposition to use with a word.

Practice 33: error correction

1 Patel states that we developed music before language (Patel 2003, cited from Bragg 2000).
2 Deforestation does not only have significant effects within one part of the world.
3 I will discuss about violence in computer games.
4 Diabetes can be broken down in two types.
5 Prevention for type one diabetes is not possible.
6 A conclusion will be drawn on whether ethics is important to business.
7 They all contribute in to making an improvement to the environment.
8 They are both at a constant state of balance.
9 There are negative effects on non-organic crops, such as a reduction in biodiversity.
10 The materials used were pertinent of the experiment.
11 One of the similarities of online and paper sources is that both forms have been written by someone.
12 In an Islamic perspective, therapeutic cloning is permissible.

5. To find or finding?

Some phrases use *to* + verb (the infinitive) and some phrases use a particular preposition followed by the verb in the '-ing' form. Try to notice how such phrases are structured. For example:

- **Infinitive:**
  The <u>failure to accept</u>
  They <u>neglect to show</u>
  They <u>expect to find</u>
  We <u>attempt to prove</u>
- **Preposition + verb –ing:**
  The <u>process of filtering</u>

The <u>success in</u> solving

He had no <u>doubt about</u> conducting the experiment

Practice 34: error correction

1 The model is capable to make accurate predictions.
2 The increase in greenhouse gases is caused by the cut down of trees on a large scale.
3 The process to utilise the waste products is complicated.
4 The failure of cells from removing sugars causes diabetes.
5 Lewes (2000) rejects the idea to use DNA as evidence of guilt.

6 *The* or nothing?

A common mistake in student writing is to miss out *the* (called the definite article) or to use it where there should be nothing. Below are notes and example sentences separated into different categories, to remind you of when to use *the* and when not to.

NB Whether to choose *the* or *a* is a separate grammatical issue and one that does not cause as many student errors as whether to use *the* or nothing.

No article

- <u>Non-specific</u> **singular countable nouns:**
  Society needs laws.
  Analysis is an important part of a report.
  Theory is as important as practice.
  Liquid usually boils when heated.
- **Uncountable nouns:**
  Research into cancer has increased.
  Progress has been made.
  You need evidence to support a claim.
- <u>Non-specific</u> **plural nouns:**
  People are complex.
  Experiments need to be reliable.
  Academic journals are useful.
- **Proper nouns (names)**
  For example, Smith / Einstein/ Freud.
- **Possessive forms of proper nouns:**
  Smith's research.
  Einstein's theory.
  Freud's idea.

The

- <u>Specific</u> **singular countable nouns (Often used with *of*):**
  The society of today.
  The analysis of the data

The theory of the firm.
The liquid in the test tube.
The theory of chaos.

- **Uncountable nouns:**
The research at the Bonn Institute.
The progress made by Smith's team is remarkable.
The evidence used to support your claim is not adequate.

- **Specific plural nouns:**
The people at the conference.
The experiments mentioned earlier in the report.
The academic journals used in the essay.

- **When only one exists:**
The nuclear transfer method.
The immune system.
The organic method.

- **Ordinals:**
The first / The second / The last . . .

- **Superlatives:**
The least / The most / The best / The highest /. . .
The most recent.

- **Specifiers:**
The main factor / The principal issue / The essential Question / The only . . . / The same report.

- **Part of a whole:**
None of the/ All of the / Some of the / Most of the / Half of the . . . / 60% of the . . .

- **Names used as adjectives:**
The Freudian theory of psychosis.

Practice 35: error correction

The sentences below have either *the* where there should be nothing, or nothing where there should be *the*.

1 There are some groups among the society which object to this research.
2 It is expected that public will benefit from this technology.
3 Researchers at University of North Texas have discovered a new drug.
4 Cloning is a controversial issue in the society.
5 Carbon dioxide mostly comes from burning of coal and other fossil fuels.
6 Third disadvantage is that it is expensive.
7 The impact of this legislation in UK has been profound.
8 For majority of people, mobile phones are now almost indispensible.
9 Author's position is neutral on this question.
10 The deforestation of Amazon Basin could lead to an increase in global temperature.
11 The study shows that immune system is extremely complex.
12 Exam timetable did not indicate what time exam was going to start.

7 Commas with that

that + no comma

Students often mistakenly put a comma after *that*. Nearly all sentences and phrases with *that* do **not** have commas because *that* introduces an essential part of the sentence. Note that you should not use a comma after *that* when introducing a quotation or a paraphrase as again, *that* introduces an essential part of the sentence.

For example:

> Prindl and Prodham (1994) suggest that 'Finance as practiced in the professions . . .'
> The evidence suggests that ageism is partly unconscious.
> It seems / appears / is clear that a strong correlation exists.
> It is important that we consider the report in detail.
> The fact is that the war did not help the country.
> The results were so surprising that they were not believed at first.
> The same research team that discovered the virus has now produced an effective vaccine.
> The experiment that was conducted by Smith's team provided useful data.
> There is only one issue that is really problematic.
> That is a situation I find hard to imagine.

that + comma

The only time *that* uses a comma is in the phrase 'that is' meaning 'namely'. Here you need to use a comma both before and after *that is*. For example:

> 'There is one problematic issue, that is, the effect of the reservoir on the local environment.'

Compare the two uses of *that* in the sentence below:

> 'There is only one issue that needs to be discussed, that is, how to best use our resources.'

Practice 36: error correction

1 It has been shown in this essay that, this is not the case.
2 It is illogical, that people think pollution is not important.
3 The fact is that, we cannot determine the outcome.
4 This essay will discuss the most important aspect of genetic research that is cloning.
5 Table 1 shows that for both homicide and suicide, males predominate over females in almost all age ranges.
6 Lenin (1914) claimed that a nation could not be truly free while it oppressed other nations.

8 Commas with *which* and *who*

Essential information clauses = no commas

If the *which / who* part of your sentence is essential information (called a defining or restrictive clause) it does not need commas around it. In the example below, the underlined part of the sentence is essential.

'Although most of the experiments failed to provide any insights, the experiment which was conducted by Smith's team provided useful data.'

Note that for this type of clause we can often use *that* or nothing.

'Although most of the experiments failed to provide any insights, the experiment (that was) conducted by Smith's team provided useful data.'

The sentence below has an essential clause introduced by *who*, so, again, there are no commas around the *who* clause.

'The authors who disagree with Carr are Esty and Collins.'

Extra information clauses = two commas

If the *which / who* part of your sentence is only additional information and could therefore be left out of the sentence (called a non-defining or non-restrictive clause) you need two commas – one before and one after the clause. Note that for this type of clause you cannot replace *which* with *that*.

'Business ethics, which has become increasingly important, can be defined as principles of behaviour as applied to business organisations.'
'Svennson and wood, who disagree with Carr, propose a dynamic model of business ethics.'

Practice 37: error correction

1 Many commentators have suggested that a system, which allows different states to have autonomy would be best.
2 There are many factors, which may affect the way a text is written.
3 Patel's data which was collected from over 300 questionnaires, showed that our proposition was correct.
4 The data, which was collected by the first research team proved not to be as reliable as that collected in later studies.
5 Condensation is the process in which a gas changes into a liquid.

9 Apostrophes

You should not use contractions in formal writing (do not =don't, they are = they're, it is / has = it's, who is = who's) so there should only be one reason to use an apostrophe in your essays; to show possession.

Note that apostrophes are only used to show possession, not to indicate a plural.

- **Possession (one country):**
  Teams from this country's scientific community developed the drug.
- **Plural (several countries):**
  Teams from seven countries developed the drug.

Apostrophes to show possession

1. If the noun is **singular**, whether it ends with an *s* or not, use **apostrophe + *s*.**

   E.g. The research of Patel = Patel's research
   The research of Kimos = Kimos's research.

2. If the noun is **plural** but does **not** end with an *s*, use **apostrophe + *s*.**

   E.g. The group of women = The women's group.

3. If the noun is **plural** and **does** end with an *s*, use <u>only</u> **the apostrophe.**

   E.g. The theory of the authors = The authors' theory. ✔.

This last rule causes the most confusion. Imagine the normal rule of 'noun followed by apostrophe + *s*' and then take off the last *s*.

   E.g. The theory of the authors = (The authors's theory) = The authors' theory.

So, we have:

   Rule 1: Jones's theory = The theory of one person (whose name ends with an *s*)
   Rule 3: The authors' theory = the theory of two or more authors.

It is becoming more common for the last *s* in rule 1 to be left off (e.g. St. James' Palace rather than St. James's Palace) but, strictly speaking, this omission of the last *s* is incorrect.

Its or *it's*?

This is a common cause of confusion. A correct example is given below.

   The title of the article is 'Expression'. = <u>Its</u> title is 'Expression'.

Writing *it's* instead of using *its* is an understandable mistake, because we normally use an apostrophe to show possession (as shown in the point on apostrophes above) and we do say *anyone's*, *anybody's*, *someone's* and *one's*. However, the possessive personal pronouns *mine*, *yours*, *his*, *hers*, *its*, *ours* and *theirs* do <u>not</u> use an apostrophe.

   Remember that *it's* is only used for the contraction of *it is* or *it has* and is too informal for essays, so you should never need to use *it's* in academic writing.

Practice 38: error correction

1 Some theologist's think that therapeutic cloning is acceptable.
2 Greenpeace states that one of it's aims is to expose threats to the environment.
3 A countries government usually resides in the capital city.
4 An employees career depends on many different factors.

5   The issue of who's concerns are most important is still unresolved.

6   People should look after their bodies health.

7   The experiment's were conducted with rigour.

8   The article does not discuss the issue in detail. It's main proposition is that the womens movement in the 1960's to 1980's was not as effective as is often thought.

9   Employee's need to wear clothes which are appropriate for their type of work.

10 The researcher's data shows that they have not proven a direct correlation.

10 Direct and indirect questions

Students sometimes make one of the following mistakes with direct or indirect questions:

- **Using too many direct questions**
  Direct questions are a little too informal for academic writing, so use them sparingly.
- **Using an indirect question with the word order of a direct question**
  Indirect questions have an introductory phrase that indicates we are questioning something, and then a second clause that has the same word order as for a non-question statement.
- **Using a question mark with an indirect question**
  An indirect question uses a full-stop.

Table 6   Direct and indirect questions

Direct question	Indirect question
What is the key issue in global warming?	We need to ask / consider / It is unclear what the key issue in global warming is.
Can mobile phones cause illness?	The question is / We need to ask whether the use of mobile phones can cause illness.
What has this research achieved?	It is unclear / We need to ask / The question remains as to what this research has achieved.

Practice 39: error correction

1   The question is whether mobile phones make us sick?

2   The issue is if this will lead to an increase in violence.

3   Research was conducted to see what was the cause of the disease.

4   It is unclear what is the problem with the strategy.

5   The question remains as to what has this research achieved.

Correcting other common types of error

This section contains real student sentences that contain various common error types, grouped under the given headings. Use these sentences to further improve your awareness of common errors and proof-reading skills.

Decide what is wrong with each sentence and then read the comments and answers on p. 139.

Practice 40: overgeneralising, oversimplifying or making unspecific or unsupported statements

1 Women are better than men.
2 People in poor countries get lower wages.
3 Portable technology is used by everyone nowadays.
4 We all see writing as having one main purpose but in fact it has many different functions.
5 Everyone knows that drugs are addictive.
6 Some people think that euthanasia should be legal but the politicians disagree.
7 In the modern world abortion is an ethically accepted advance.
8 Millions of women risk their lives to stop unwanted pregnancy.
9 The majority of men gamble in their twenties.
10 There are hundreds of women attacked each year.
11 There is more demand for organ transplants than ever before.
12 The UK has an increasing number of drug users.

Practice 41: not explaining yourself clearly

1 The Mediterranean which is the dirtiest sea in the world is caused by tourism.
2 I have chosen to discuss cloning because I want to put forward the major advance technology and why I consider cloning to be prohibited.
3 Cloning animals has been debated between scientists, politicians and the general public on how cloning has been treated and how they might clone humans.
4 The nephron has five main parts for the process to work.
5 Academic writing is a form of writing that students adapt to their work.
6 Personal writing is more of your own feelings.
7 This is a holiday development for the country.

8 Deoxygenated blood is pumped from the heart into the lungs and vice versa.
9 Luchens (2006) found that some children are allowed to watch violent films by their parents, and that they behave more aggressively after watching them.
10 The government hopes that the legislation will protect the public so that the fatalities between 1988 and 2001 can be avoided.

Practice 42: missing words or phrases

1 When deforestation, the Earth's photosynthetic capacity decreases and cannot remove carbon dioxide.
2 A good dictionary is to find out the meaning of a word.
3 'Cultural baggage' is tourists carrying their own values.
4 There is, for example, between diet and disease.
5 The process continues to the final stage which in the second coiled tubule.
6 Organ transplantation has risks involving the rejection of the immune system.
7 Some consider homosexuality to be morally wrong and should therefore be classified illegal.
8 Research shows that by regulating your emotions, for example pretending to be happier than you are.
9 In this case we have to search each word that we do not know, at least a rough meaning.
10 Is clear from this data that further studies need to be conducted.

Practice 43: extra words or phrases

1 Although there are many differences between formal and informal writing.
2 This essay will examine how businesses are run, bearing in mind with the ethical issues.
3 Type two diabetes it can be managed by having a healthy diet and lifestyle.
4 The first stage in ultrafiltration which occurs in the glomerulus.
5 According to many Catholics, they believe life begins at conception.

Practice 44: wrong phrase order

1 Animal testing has been disputed, whether it is right or wrong.
2 There is a natural connection between aspects of spoken language and the cultural identity of a group, such as accent, vocabulary and discourse patterns.
3 Developing countries are trying to attract foreign skilled professionals such as China.
4 Deforestation reduces the earth's capacity to regulate the atmosphere and thereby its ability to absorb carbon dioxide.
5 Moreover, the different types of stem cells will be discussed and their respective capabilities.

Appendices

Answers to practice exercises

Section A1

Practice 1

1 Reliable information for general issues on disability but may be biased. Not an academic source.
2 Not reliable and not an academic source.
3 Reliable and an academic source but 2002 is quite old for such a topic, which decreases how reliable the information will be.
4 a. Reliable for some ideas on issues but may be biased and inaccurate. Not an academic source.
  b. Reliable and an academic source.
  c. Quite reliable but not an academic source.
5 Reliable for introducing main issues but not an academic source. Also the booklet is quite old for this topic and this further decreases how reliable the source is for information on animal cloning.
6 Probably reliable as information from businesses but not an academic source. You would also need to check when the website was updated.
7 Not reliable and not an academic source.
8 Reliable as information from businesses but not an academic source.
9 Reliable for general discussion and ideas but not peer-reviewed and therefore not academically reliable. You should find and use articles from the Centre's 'Journal of Ethics' for academic sources.
10 Not reliable and will be biased, as it seems to be written by a pressure group. Not an academic source.

Section A2

Practice 2

Questioning

Carr assumes that businessmen are ethical in their private lives – this may not be true. He also assumes that all businesses operate in the same way, that they all have separate ethical standards from private ones and that you always have to choose between losing and lying. This may not be true – there may be other options and other types of business model.

Evaluating

His style is quite persuasive – I instinctively feel he is partly right – but he is very cynical and oversimplifies. He gives no evidence for his views and doesn't try to be objective or look at opposing evidence. His argument isn't very well ordered, as it is continuous opinion rather than a developed argument. I agree with Carr that some people feel they do need to lie in business but not that this is always the case or that business ethics are totally separate from social norms – not true nowadays?

I will use Carr as a key source to show an expert who opposes the idea of business ethics and I will then criticise his argument by giving opposing evidence from Svensson and Wood.

Locating

Carr's article seems to have been radical and important at the time (1968) because a lot of other texts still refer to it. In terms of business ethics he is definitely in the 'no' camp. His article is very dated now and things have moved on since then – now there is more legislation on regulation of corporate behaviour, corporate transparency and accountability and more emphasis on ethics and sustainability.

Section A3

Practice 3

Example notes

	Carr, A. Z. (1968) 'Is business bluffing ethical?' *Harvard Business Review*, 46(1), pp. 143–153. Notes written on 23/10/2012
p. 145. main point.	Ethics of bus. are like the rules of poker (distrust) – diff. from 'civilised human relationships'.
p. 145. (bottom) Not true?	Most busmn. are ethical in private lives, but at work they stop being 'private citizens' + follow the *different* ethical rules of bus.
p. 148.	The image that bus. gives of using ethics from private life e.g."'Sound ethics is good for business'" is only a 'self-serving' + profit making deception, not a true ethical position.
p.153. (Conclusion) Not true now/all businesses? – other choices?	'To be a winner, a man must play to win'. Busmn will sometimes have to choose betwn. losing and 'bluffing' (lying) like Poker. To succeed he will have to 'bluff hard'.
2nd main point.	'Bluffing' is 'integral' to business.

NB 'Sound ethics is good for business' is a quotation used by Carr in his article (Carr does not give the source of the quotation). The student has made this clear in his notes by using single and then also double quotation marks to show that Carr is quoting someone else.

Section A4

Practice 4

1 This quotation is not special in what it says or how it is expressed. The student should have given this information in their own words as far as possible, for example: Kzanty (2004) states that organs such as the lungs, pancreas and heart are used in transplantation.
2 This information is common fact and knowledge so can be given in the essay without attribution to the author.
3 The quotation partially contradicts the student's point that transplants save lives.
4 The quotation is about the student's first point (improvements in transplantation techniques using animal organs) not about the point that is immediately in front of the quotation, that patients do not have to wait for transplants.
5 The quotation is not introduced clearly – it does not explain which trial or study is referred to or who 'everyone' is.

Practice 5

1 There are no quotation marks and no in-essay reference. This is plagiarism.
2 There is an in-essay reference but no quotation marks. This is plagiarism.
3 There are quotation marks but no in-essay reference. This might be seen as plagiarism.
4 There are quotation marks and an in-essay reference, but the authors' names should not be in brackets and the page number is missing. The page number must be included for quotations if you use the author/date system of referencing.

Practice 6

1 The student has added the word *business* to the original wording. She should either take this word out or put it in square brackets e.g. [business].
2 The student has taken out the words *synonymous with* from the original text. She should use ellipsis (three dots with a space in between each one) to show this. For example: *'good ethics is . . . good management' (p. 2)*.
3 The topic words *good ethics* are used twice, once in the introductory sentence and again in the quotation. They should be used in one or the other but not both. For example:

> This idea is expressed succinctly by Collins (1994) in his discussion of good ethics when he states that '[It] is synonymous with good management' (p. 2).

4 The full stop at the end of the quotation is inside the quotation marks. It should come outside the quotation marks after the page number brackets.

Correct version of the extract using a numeric system of referencing

> My first proposition is that businesses actually *need* to behave in an ethical

manner. This idea is expressed succinctly by Collins when he states that 'good ethics is synonymous with good management' (1).

Works Cited
J. W. Collins (1994) 'Is business ethics an oxymoron?' *Business Horizons*; 37(5):1–8.

Section A5

Practice 7

1 The paraphrase itself is good as it is written in the student's own words. However, there are no in-essay references and so this counts as plagiarism.
2 The paraphrase is rewritten in the student's own words and has an initial in-essay reference. However, there it is no reference reminder phrase in the second sentence and so it is not clear whether this sentence is an idea from the student or from the source. This could be seen as plagiarism.
3 There is only one in-essay reference, given at the end of the paragraph. It is therefore not clear whether the first sentence is the student's idea or an idea from the source – this could be seen as plagiarism. It is much better to integrate a reference into the first sentence of a paraphrase and then to use reference reminder phrases.
4 This paraphrase consists of one sentence copied Cox and a second sentence copied from the Maier, Blakemore and Koivisto text. The sentences have been stitched together without the use of quotation marks and without adequate referencing. This is plagiarism.

Example of an acceptable paraphrase of the Cox extract

Using the author/date style of in-essay referencing:

> Cox (2003) suggests that advising caution in the use of mobile phones is an example of a typical approach to the fear of a possible health risk which may be of a serious nature. He states that such an approach may have negative consequences, but is taken because although there may in fact be no health risk, this has not yet been proven.

Using the number/footnote style of in-essay referencing:

> Cox (1) suggests that advising caution in the use of mobile phones is an example of a typical approach to the fear of a possible health risk which may be of a serious nature. He states that such an approach may have negative consequences, but is taken because although there may in fact be no health risk, this has not yet been proven.

Works Cited
Cox, D.R. (2003) 'Communication of risk: health hazards from mobile phones' *Journal of the Royal Statistical Society: Series A (Statistics in Society)*, 166(2), pp. 214–246.

Practice 8

Example of an acceptable paraphrase

Using the author/date style of in-essay referencing:

> According to the Telecommunications Reports (2005), the mobile phone industry states that there is no evidence to suggest phones damage the health of users and that the number of UK users in 2005 (50 million) had doubled in five years.

Using the numeric style of in-essay referencing:

> According to the Telecommunications Reports (1), the mobile phone industry states that there is no evidence to suggest phones damage the health of users and that the number of UK users in 2005 (50 million) had doubled in five years.

> ### Works Cited
> Telecommunications Reports. 'U.K. Finds 'No Hard Evidence' of Cellphone Health Risk'. 2005, 71(2):19–20.

Section A6

Practice 10

Example of a one-sentence summary of the Dobson text

> Dobson (2010) describes how the UK Department of Culture, Media and Sport supports all levels of sport but particularly sport for children, with the aim of encouraging life-long physical activity and good health.

Example of a two-sentence summary of the Dobson text

> Dobson (2010) describes the main aims of the UK Department of Culture, Media and Sport as not only funding and supporting sport of all types and at all levels, but in particular, of increasing the amount of sporting opportunity and activity for school age children. Dobson states that the DCMS hopes its specific targets in this area will lead to an improvement in the long-term physical health of the UK population.

Section B1

Practice 12

1 *Studying / examining / investigating* the possible . . . *Undergo* is only used for the people or things to which the experiment or event happen. For example: 'The patient will undergo two operations.' It is not used with *about*.
2 *Show / prove / illustrate*. It is already clear that cigarettes are harmful – the evidence is to show to what extent (how much) they damage health.
3 Suggests / implies. The word *impose* has a very different meaning.
4 *states / suggests / shows* (other verbs are also possible).The verb *mention* is only used to refer to a minor point and therefore should not be used when summarising.

5 Conceived. This means when an idea is first thought of. *Perceived* means 'thought of / viewed in a particular way'.

6 Invented. *Established* means 'to set up something that continues' e.g. a company, charity or theory. *Discovered* would also be incorrect, as this verb can only be used when something is first found that already existed.

7 Conveyed. This means 'communicated'. *Portrayed* means 'represented or described in a particular way'.

8 The student has used the wrong verb (*implied*) to introduce the quotation. The quote from Murtaz is a clear statement, not something which he has only implied but not openly said. The student could have used a verb such as *stated, argued or asserted.*

9 The verb *claim* is usually used to show that you do *not* agree with what the author says in the quotation. However, the student goes on to say that her essay will show that she thinks the statement in the quotation is correct. A more appropriate verb would have been a positive verb such as *show* or a neutral verb such as *state* or *suggest.*

10 Discusses the portrayal . . . The verbs *discuss, describe* and *define* in the active tense are not followed by a preposition (e.g. *about / in / at / on*). They are followed by a noun only (e.g. 'I will discuss the issue' / 'Smith describes the effects').

11 This essay will *argue that there is a link* between regulating emotions and job satisfaction. The verbs *argue* and *conclude* can only be followed by *that + sentence.*

12 Emotion regulation is defined as hiding or trying to modify your emotions. Verbs such as *describe* and *define* used in the passive tense for definitions are followed by *as* not *that.*

Section B2

Practice 13

1 There are several different <u>opinions / views / points of view</u> as to what constitutes an offence.

2 Brenner is a strong <u>advocate of</u> women's rights.

3 A primary <u>objection from</u> some religious groups to IVF from of some religious is that it uses external fertilisation.

4 Balkin (2002) <u>opposes / is opposed to</u> sex segregation in schools in that it is a diversion from more important educative issues.

5 Many pressure groups have strong <u>views on</u> embryonic research.

6 Some people <u>take the view that</u> since they already pay income tax, they should not be additionally taxed on interest from savings.

7 This report has outlined the <u>arguments against / reasons for opposing</u> animal testing.

8 Mueller (2011) states that people often <u>reject</u> creative ideas because they are scared of change.

9 The current government in Mexico is adopting an expansionary economic <u>stance / position.</u>

10 A <u>counterargument</u> to humour being used to show dominance is that it is used to relieve social tension.

Section B3

Practice 14

1 <u>In my view, / I suggest that</u> the issue of global warming is not as serious as the media portrays.
2 Kerlinger (1969) <u>states</u> that '*Science* is a misused and misunderstood word' (p. 1127).
3 It has been <u>claimed / suggested / stated / proven </u>that computer games can be used to educate children.
4 Smith (2009) has criticised Ramone's work <u>for</u> being overcomplicated.
5 Karl Marx <u>rejected</u> capitalism as a positive system for social development.
6 According <u>to</u> Gilchrist, we need to re-evaluate how we perceive risk-taking heroines, particularly those who are also mothers.
7 Kroll <u>uses / / gives / / quotes / / paraphrases </u>Frie as an example of how early approaches to second-language learning saw teaching writing as a secondary to speech.
8 The research team <u>acknowledges</u> that their data is incomplete and that further studies are needed.
9 According to <u>Reynolds (2000)</u> there is no strong evidence of long-term damage to health.
10 As Collins (1994) <u>states,</u> 'good ethics is synonymous with good management.' (p. 2).

Practice 15

(The underlined words are given in section B3)
    There are three main <u>distinct</u> theories of job satisfaction. One model states that both job type and employee personality are central to determining job satisfaction. This is because organisational structure influences the characteristics of a job, and jobs with particular characteristics attract people with particular personality attributes. These attributes in turn affect how satisfied a person will be with their job (Oldham and Hackman, 1981). <u>In contrast</u> to this model, the dispositional approach sees a person's disposition (or personality) as the most important element in determining the level of job satisfaction, regardless of job type (Staw, Bell and Clausen, 1986). Finally, Locke 's theory of job satisfaction <u>differs from</u> both of the above, as it regards what a person wants to do in a job and how far these goals are achieved as the main factors that determine job satisfaction (Locke, 1968).

Section B4

Practice 16

1 The new company is extremely <u>innovative</u>.
2 The National Bureau of Economic Research has been <u>of great benefit to</u> the field of economics in recent years.
3 I will look at both the theoretical and <u>substantive</u> implications of recent research on the consequences of job insecurity.

4 Lupton (1998) <u>claims</u> that the public is interested in health news. However, I will argue that media coverage in this area does not necessarily indicate genuine public interest.

5 Oswald's research <u>supports</u> the idea that having a job is more significant for happiness than being wealthy.

6 Jack, James and Roger's explanation of the effect of caffeine on performance seems to me the most <u>plausible</u> because . . .

7 The <u>validity</u> of this belief is called into question by recent evidence.

8 Although the survey is <u>extensive / wide-ranging</u>, it fails to look at applications of learning curve theory.

9 Carr (1968) uses the <u>illuminating</u> analogy of a poker player to demonstrate his position on business ethics.

10 Importantly, the findings are <u>consistent with</u> those of previous studies.

Section B5

Practice 17

1 To state that cancer is caused by obesity is an <u>oversimplification.</u>

2 The study <u>claimed / maintained / asserted / suggested</u> . . . that mass media can be used to educate children but this was not borne out by the evidence.

3 The conclusion is <u>contradicted by</u> the data given earlier in the paper.

4 Tanen (2000) <u>claimed / maintained / contended / asserted (stated)</u> that visual imprinting occurs in infancy. However, this was shown to be incorrect by later studies.

5 Bijal (2002) <u>fails to consider</u> the fact that in most urban areas rich and poor sometimes live in close proximity.

6 Smith's study is <u>limited</u> because the sample size is extremely small.

7 The experiment was conducted according to a standard / precise <u>method</u> in order to ensure reliability.

8 The arguments in Bazer's article have a strong Eurocentric <u>bias / are highly biased towards</u> Europe.

9 Hooper's theory of the origin of the HIV virus <u>suffers from</u> lack of evidence.

10 The theory was <u>discredited</u> in 2001, when it was shown that there was no evidence to support it.

Practice 18

Formal essay paragraph written from the informal critical analysis of the Carr article. (Underlined words are presented in the B5 example sentences.)

Although Carr's argument may <u>seem</u> persuasive, <u>it has several flaws.</u> His <u>view lacks evidence</u> and he <u>does not take into account the fact that</u> business decisions are not always as clear cut as he suggests. He also <u>fails to consider</u> other potential business models and practices and <u>ignores the fact that</u> total separation of business from society is not possible.

SectionB6

Practice 19

	Original extract	Student paraphrase
Synonyms	*not equivalent* *social rules* *primarily* *morally contestable issues*	*not synonymous* *acceptable behaviour* *mainly* *open to different interpretations*
Word form	*law* *regulations* *overlap (n)*	*legality* *regulates* *overlap (v.)*
Tense		No tense changes
Order of information	**1.** Overlap but not equivalent 2. BE primarily concerned with issues not covered by law	1. BE primarily concerned with issues not covered by law 2. Overlap but not equivalent
Sentence structure	Most sentence patterns and structures have been changed.	

Practice 20

Oswald's research challenges the common assumption made in developed countries that economic growth and increase in individual income make people happier. He suggests that although many of us believe this to be the case, evidence shows that such increases in wealth do not lead to any significant increase in how happy we feel (Oswald 1997).

Section B7

Practice 21

Suggested answers (other alternatives are possible).

1 . . . detrimental to / has negative effects on . . . (avoid using *good* and *bad)*
2 . . . ,which should not be allowed to continue.
3 . . . resolved / solved / dealt with by . . .
4 There is no evidence that . . .
5 The fundamental issue is whether you have the ability to regulate your emotions.
6 . . . are complex / difficult to understand.
7 The most important / fundamental point is that . . .

8 . . . isolated from society.
9 If this (trend) continues . .
10 They were surprised / confused by the results.
11 Organ transplantation is not effective.
12 Patients should not be treated like this.
13 They should not be interfered with / disturbed.
14 It will not help us. / It will not solve the problem / situation.
15 This situation is very different.
16 . . . cannot continue.
17 Globalisation is likely to have negative effects on the human species.
18 There are different kinds of businesses such as private, public and non-profit
making.
19 It's a serious / significant problem.
20 The most important action / step to take is to . . .

Practice 22

Cote and Morgan demonstrated that as they predicted, suppressing unpleasant
emotions leads to a decrease in job satisfaction and so an increase in intention to quit.
Their findings also suggest that an increase in pleasant emotions will increase job
satisfaction because it increases positive social interaction and better responses from
colleagues and customers.

Section C1

Practice 23

1 According to Reynolds (2000), . . .
2 According to Padash (2000), . . .
3 Marchais (1984) discusses . . .
4 Locke (1997) suggests that . . .
5 Inadequate reference. The author (or organisation if no author) and year should be
given, as with any reference. Words such as *article* or *book* should never be used as
part of a bracketed reference.
6 The author should be referred to, as with any other reference – not the website. For
example, 'McDermot (1999) has drawn attention to the fact that more research
needs to be done.'
7 You should not normally give the title of the book, and details such as edition
numbers should not be used in an in-essay reference (in fact *Economics* is only part
of the book title; if you do want to include the title it must be accurate and in full).
The correct reference should be (Sloman 1997).
8 Inadequate reference. If you want to include the title of an article or book you must
also give the author and year:
These factors are discussed by Smith (1990) in the article titled 'Biometric data of
the future'.
9 The year must be included and there should not be quotation marks around the
authors' names.

10 There is no in-essay reference.
11 Do not use bold, underline, italics or any other type of variant font for in-essay references (italics are sometimes used for a book / article titles).
12 The author and year should be used rather than the article title. If the article title is included it should be with initial capitals and either in quotation marks or in italics.

Practice 24

1 In my view, . . .
According to is only used when referring to other people. For example: 'According to Nitka (1980) . . .'
2 Kerlinger (1969) states that:
3 Jones (2002) demonstrates / shows that governments . . .
Don't mention details such as a book having been written or published.
4 As Collins (1994) states / suggests / claims . . .
5 These factors are discussed in the article 'Dying to be thin'.
6 The issue . . . is controversial.
Don't write about your reading / research process unless this is a specific part of the assignment.

Practice 25

1 Cote and Morgan (2002) showed that . . .
2 Coates and Bailey (1995) examined . . .
3 According to the *New Scientist* (8 / 1 / 2005) people are still not . . .
4 As Crème and Lea (1997) have stated, the gap between . . .
5 According to Smith (2000), the problem is widespread.

Practice 26

1 It is unclear where the quotation ends as there are three quotation marks. There is also an incorrect extra bracket at the end of the sentence.
2 Knowles (1998) states that 'groups work more efficiently' (p.64).
NB – this information is not special enough to use as a quotation and should have been paraphrased.
3 This quotation does not fit grammatically with the sentence and also contains information that is not special enough to quote. There should also be a bracket around the year of publication: Jones (2006) states that it is crucial that we understand the various causes of mental illness.

Section C2

Practice 27

1 differentiates	v.
2 per cent	n.
3 tourists	n.
4 advantages	n.
5 continues	v.

6 contribution   n.
7 clearly   adv.
8 religious beliefs   adj. + noun
9 confidentiality   n.
10 To conclude   v.
11 the risk to health.
   (**NB** in lists, all parts of the list should follow the same grammatical pattern, in this case noun phrases – the expense, the length, the risk.)
10 potential   adj.

Practice 28

1 has increased. (the number of + has)
2 report
3 shows
4 helps
5 has been (malicious software + has)
6 differ
7 has
8 implies
9 has (the use of + has)
10 Much research is
11 is reabsorbed
12 is the weight.
13 Much / A great deal of information

Practice 29

1 For example, 'the risk to the health of the patients is high'.
2 Firstly, I will discuss the positive aspects of drug therapy.
3 An increasing number of people find it difficult to get a job.
4 Guideline daily amounts on food labels are an alternative to the traffic light system of labelling.
5 The majority of drug users are aged between eighteen and thirty.

Practice 30

1 Although there are several advantages, there are also drawbacks.
2 Our data, which shows a direct correlation between lack of light and depression, is flawed.
3 The theory cannot be viewed as valid, as they have found that it contains several inconsistencies.
4 As well as giving out benefits to families in poverty, the government needs a longer-term strategy.
5 The defendant has not been named owing to fears about levels of media attention.
6 Even though the participants suffered mild side-effects, the drug passed the initial trial.

Practice 31

1 Dorkin argues that
2 Herschel points out that
3 Donne states that
4 Lockheart demonstrates that
5 The study suggests that . . .
6 Hanson claims that . . . (no *that* would be acceptable in less formal writing)

Practice 32

1 Cote and Morgan have shown that emotion regulation influences job satisfaction and that amplifying positive emotions increases positive interaction with both colleagues and customers. However, they have found that there is not an opposite correlation, that is, that job satisfaction affects emotion regulation.
2 The business decisions managers take can have significant implications but / yet most managers do not have training in business ethics.
  OR
  The business decisions managers take can have significant implications. However, most managers do not have training in business ethics.
3 The worldwide web is a constantly developing technology; it has many advantages for society.
  OR
  The worldwide web is a constantly developing technology and it has many advantages for society.
4 Lupton (1998) claims that the public is interested in health news . / ; However, I will argue that media coverage does not indicate genuine public interest.
5 Wolf (2008) argues that business should not concern itself with social consequences . / ; On the other hand, Svensson and Wood claim that business and society are co-dependent.

Practice 33

1 cited in
2 effects on
3 I will discuss violence . . . (*discuss* is never followed by about)
4 broken down into
5 Prevention of
6 be drawn as to whether
7 They all contribute to making
8 in a constant state of balance.
9 negative effects of
10 pertinent / relevant to the experiment.
11 the similarities between
12 From an Islamic perspective

Practice 34

1 capable of making

2 is caused by the cutting down
3 The process of utilising the waste
4 The failure of cells to remove
5 rejects the idea of using DNA

Practice 35

1 among society
2 the public
3 the University of North Texas
4 in society
5 the burning of coal
6 The third disadvantage
7 the UK
8 the majority of people
9 The author's position
10 the Amazon Basin
11 the immune system
12 The exam timetable . . . the exam

Practice 36

1 It has been shown in this essay that this is not the case.
2 It is illogical that people think pollution is not important.
3 The fact is that we cannot determine the outcome.
4 This essay will discuss the most important aspect of genetic research, that is, cloning.
5 Correct
6 Correct

Practice 37

1 Many commentators have suggested that a system which allows different states to have autonomy would be best.
2 There are many factors that / which may affect the way a text is written.
   (You cannot use nothing instead of *which* / *that* because the pronoun refers to *the factors* which is the subject of the clause, not the object.)
3 Patel's data, which was collected from over 300 questionnaires, showed that our proposition was correct.
   OR
   Patel's data, collected from over 300 questionnaires, showed that our proposition was correct.
4 The data which was collected by the first research team proved not to be as reliable as that collected in later studies.
5 Correct.

Practice 38

1 theologists
2 its

3 A country's
4 employee's
5 whose
6 body's
7 experiments
8 Its main proposition is that the women's . . .
9 Employees
10 The researchers' data

Practice 39

1 The question is whether mobile phones make us sick.
2 The issue is whether this will lead to an increase in violence.
3 Research was conducted to identify the cause of the disease.
4 We have not identified the problem with the strategy. /
  It is unclear what the problem with the strategy is.
5 The question remains as to what this research has achieved.

Section C3

Practice 40

Sentences 1–7 are examples of overgeneralisation or oversimplification. You can't use words or phrases such as *women, people, everyone, we all, the politicians* and *in the modern world* because it is rarely the case that something applies to everyone or that we all know or think the same way. Statements 1–7 all need qualification and / or specification, such as *some women, the majority of manual workers . . . compared to western countries, many UK liberal politicians* and *most people are aware that . . .*

It would be even better if these statements contained qualification, specific examples and a specific source as supporting evidence.

For example: 'In some respects, many women seem to have superior skills or attributes to men, such as the ability to empathise. This is supported by Smith (2000) who shows that . . . '

Statements 8–12 are not overgeneralisations (although vague numbers such as *millions* should be avoided) but they all need qualification, a specific context and use of source to support the claim.

For example: 'There is evidence to suggest that in many Canadian cities, the majority of Chinese men in their twenties gamble to some extent. A study conducted by Papineau in 2005 showed that . . .'

Practice 41

1 The pollution in the Mediterranean, which is the dirtiest sea in the world, is caused by tourism.
2 I have chosen to discuss cloning because I want to discuss the major advances in this technology and why cloning should be prohibited.
3 The issue of cloning animals and possibly humans has been debated by scientists, politicians and the general public.

4 The nephron has five main parts / components which / that are all essential for the process to work.
5 Academic writing is a form of writing that / which students need to adapt to and use in their work.
6 Personal writing is more concerned with personal feelings than with objective facts.
7 This is a development in the country's tourism industry.
8 Comment: *Vice versa* can only be used for a direct reversal of two things. In the student sentence it would mean that deoxygenated blood is also pumped from the lungs into the heart. This is not correct, as only oxygenated blood flows back from lungs to heart. The sentence should therefore be, for example:

> 'Deoxygenated blood is pumped from the heart through the lungs and then the oxygenated blood flows back from the lungs into the heart.'
> NB *vice* is spelt with a *c* (not *visa*).

9 The use of the pronoun *they* means that the reader is not sure whether it is the children or the parents who behave aggressively. Also, the pronoun *them* could refer to films or to parents.

> If there is more than one subject in a sentence, use the full noun instead of a pronoun, or alter the sentence so that there is no other subject noun between the noun and the pronoun is refers to.

> For example: 'Luchens (2006) found that some children are allowed by their parents to watch violent films, and that these children behave more aggressively after watching such films.'

> OR 'Luchens (2006) found that some parents allow their children to watch violent films and that they behave more aggressively after watching them.'

10 The government hopes that the legislation will protect the public so that a repetition of the level of fatalities that occurred between 1988 and 2001 can be avoided.

Practice 42

Alternative answers are possible for some sentences.

1 When deforestation *occurs*, the Earth's photosynthetic capacity decreases and it cannot *remove* carbon dioxide.
2 A good dictionary is *used* to find . . .
3 'Cultural baggage' is *when* tourists *carry* their own values *with them*.
4 For example, 'There is, for example a *link / a correlation* between diet and disease.
5 . . . the final stage which *takes place in* the second coiled tubule.
6 . . . the rejection of *the organ by* the immune system.
7 . . . morally wrong and *that it* should therefore be classified illegal.
8 . . . to be happier than you are, *you will increase job satisfaction.*
9 . . . to search *for* each word that we do not know, *to gain* at least . . .
10 *It* is clear that . . .

Practice 43

1 *Although* should be deleted, or a second clause added to the sentence.
2 *with* should be deleted.
3 *It* should be deleted.
4 The first stage in ultrafiltration occurs in the glomerulus.
5 According to many Catholics, life begins at conception.

Practice 44

1 Whether animal testing is right or wrong has been disputed.
  (It would be better to write this as, for example: 'The rights and wrongs of animal testing have been debated').
2 There is a natural connection between aspects of spoken language, for example accent, vocabulary and discourse patterns, and the cultural identity of a group.
3 Developing countries, such as China, are trying to attract skilled professionals from other countries.
4 Deforestation reduces the earth's capacity to absorb carbon dioxide and thereby regulate the atmosphere.
5 Moreover, the different types of stem cells and their respective capabilities will be discussed.

Definitions of terms used in How to Use your Reading In your Essays

abstract – a summary (usually of about 100 words) of an article, report or book that includes the main argument or problem, the procedures, results and conclusion. Abstracts are always written by the authors of the source and are normally used by readers to decide whether they want to read the whole text.

academic/scholarly journal – a journal that contains reliable, peer-reviewed articles of good quality.

academic source – a book, article or other type of text that has been peer-reviewed and/or is written by experts in the subject.

argument – a sequence of reasons to support a particular theory, proposition or point of view.

bibliographic details – the full details of a source given at the end of a written text.

citation – information on who wrote something, given within the piece of writing. *Citation* is also sometimes used to mean a quotation.

close paraphrase – when most of the words of the original source are used with only small changes. Close paraphrase should only be used when taking notes.

critical thinking – the process of identifying the argument of a text and then breaking it down and evaluating it to decide whether it is based on correct assumptions, logical reasoning and sound evidence.

digest – a brief summary of one source or a compilation of summaries of many different sources on a particular topic. It can be written by the authors themselves or by a third party.

e.g. – abbreviation of the Latin *exempli gratia* meaning 'for example'. Note that writing 'e.g.' as 'eg' (without a full stop after each letter) is becoming increasingly acceptable. Note also that 'e.g.' and 'i.e.' have very different meanings (see 'i.e.' below).

et al. – abbreviation of the Latin *et alii* meaning 'and others'. Used for in-essay referencing when a source has more than two authors.

evaluation/to evaluate – to reflect on and assess the information and argument of something.

extract – a section of text.

ibid. – from the Latin *ibidem* meaning 'in the same place'. Used as an in-essay reference to indicate that the source is exactly the same as the one previously given.

i.e. – from the Latin *id est* meaning 'that is'. In writing *i.e.* is used to mean 'that is to say' or 'in other words'. Be careful not to confuse *i.e.* with *e.g.* With *i.e.* you must state the complete idea or complete set of items. With *e.g.* you only give one or two examples of the set.

literature search – the process of looking for, finding and selecting relevant material and sources.

literature review – summarising and comparing the key authors and sources on a particular topic or issue.

paraphrase / to paraphrase – re-expressing all the information and ideas from a section of text in your own words and style.

peer-review – the system by which articles are checked for quality and accuracy by relevant academic experts before being published.

plagiarism / to plagiarise – presenting someone else's ideas, information, wording or style (or any combination of these) as your own, from a whole text down to just one sentence or long phrase. Plagiarism also includes claiming that work done jointly with other students is solely your own (this is called collusion). Plagiarism can occur accidentally due to poor writing and referencing, or on purpose to gain a particular advantage or benefit.

primary source – the first, original source of information or ideas, for example the original report written by the person who conducted an experiment, or the original article or book written by an author.

quotation / to quote – a phrase, sentence or section of a source given in your writing word for word, without any changes from the original.

research – any type of organised search, study, investigation or work that is done in order to develop ideas and knowledge.

scan – to look at or read something quickly in order to identify key points or to assess whether something is relevant for more detailed reading.

school of thought – a way of thinking, set of beliefs, or accepted theory or approach, e.g. behaviourism, socialism, Marxism, feminism.

secondary source – a source which writes about, discusses or uses a previously written primary source.

text – a word used to describe any written document when focussing on the content rather than the type of document.

Complete student essay on business ethics

Outline what business ethics is and discuss whether it is important.

(2,000 words)

Over the past couple of decades, the ethical credentials of businesses appear to have become an explicit factor in consumer choice. An illustration of this is the current number of publications in the UK that give consumers information on what are called 'ethical companies'. The Ethical Company Organisation (2012) for example, lists businesses ranging from pet food producers and florists to banks and stationery companies, and the organisation offers companies 'ethical accreditation'. The UK ethical market is valued at over 30 billion euros per year, and there are currently over 14,000 books and 4 million web entries related to business ethics (The Co-operative Bank 2008, cited in Crane and Matten 2010). In this essay I will first describe what business ethics is, and will then consider whether it is important as a concept and as an aspect of business activity.

There are numerous, overlapping definitions of business ethics. Shaw and Barry (2007) define it as 'the study of what constitutes right and wrong (or good and bad) human conduct in a business context' (p. 25). Another definition describes business ethics as the 'principles and standards that guide behaviour in the world of business' (Ferrell et al. 2002, p. 6). It is important to emphasise here that business ethics is not synonymous with legality. There is some overlap between law and ethics, but legislation usually only regulates the lowest level of acceptable behaviour (Crane and Matten 2010). In addition, as Trevino and Nelson (2010) point out, the law is limited in what it can do to prevent unacceptable actions, because legislation follows rather than precedes trends in behaviour. Business ethics then, as Crane and Matten state, is mainly concerned with areas of conduct that are *not* specifically covered by law and that are therefore open to different interpretations, a fact that means a particular behaviour may be legal albeit viewed as unethical.

Another important distinction to make is that ethics is not equivalent to general morality. Crane and Matten explain that although morals are a basic premise of ethics, ethics and ethical theory go a step further because they focus on how morals can be *applied* to produce explicit standards and rules for particular contexts, of which business is one. I define business ethics here then, as any aspect of business standards and/or behaviour that directly or indirectly relates to moral principles. Importantly, an action can be considered ethical regardless of whether it arises from a genuine desire to be moral or merely as a result of profit-driven motives.

There are diverse opinions as to whether ethics does have a valid place in a business. These views range from a clear 'yes' and the argument that ethical behaviour should be a core value in any organisation, to a definite 'no' and the argument that ethics should not play any part in a business. Opponents of the concept of ethics in business include those who claim that making a profit is the only responsibility a business has to society (Friedman 1970, cited in Fisher and Lovell 2003). Others such as Wolf (2008) share this view, and Prindl and Prodham (1994) suggest that 'Finance as practiced in the professions and in industry is seen as a value-neutral positive discipline, promoting efficiency without regard to the social consequences which follow from its products' (p. 3). Carr (1968) uses the analogy of a poker game to argue that a successful businessman needs to play by the rules of the industry and that these include 'bluffing' as an acceptable form of behaviour. He suggests that what is in effect lying is merely part of legitimate business strategy, and that business rules do not need to take account of personal or social principles. In this short essay I am going to use three points to argue against Carr, Wolf and others of a similar view, and propose that business success does not and should not exclude ethical behaviour. I suggest that business ethics is extremely important for the study of business, the conduct of businesses and moreover for society as a whole.

My first proposition is that businesses actually *need* to behave in an ethical manner. This idea is expressed succinctly by Collins (1994) when he states that 'good ethics is synonymous with good management' (p. 2). Collins states that if managers only concern themselves with profit, they will become 'dysfunctional'. This is because any business is made up of people; employees, customers and other stakeholders. He suggests that if businesses do not operate with a degree of trust, co-operation and consideration both inside the organisation and externally, they will in fact be putting constraints on profitability. This idea of the interdependence of a business organisation is also supported by Shaw and Barry (2007), Green (1994), Fritzsche (2005) and Svensson and Wood (2008).

Secondly, and perhaps most importantly, I suggest that ethical behaviour in business is essential because organisations are an integral part of society and that their actions have enormous consequences for the national and global community. Increasingly, various types of stakeholders (customers, as demonstrated by the statistics given in the introduction, governments, and even some financial markets) expect businesses to behave well. This is particularly true perhaps of multinationals, whose activities involve the use of resources and employees in other countries. Increasingly, 'citizens of first world societies expect their corporations to display integrity in their international business dealings' (Svensson and Wood 2008 p.312). A growing number of companies accordingly extol their ethical credentials. One very well-known and arguably extreme example of this is The Body Shop. Their main strapline is 'We're different because of our values' ('The Body Shop: Values and Campaigns') and they have a whole website devoted to telling consumers about their values and campaigns. This site lists a vast range of ethical areas that includes responsible sourcing, promoting employee well-being and effecting social change. As Esty (2007) points out, companies are now expected to publish reports on aspects of their activities such as greenhouse gas emission and energy performance, and if they do not reach expected ethical targets, their reputation and possibly also their financial investment prospects are likely to suffer – a point that links back to the idea of businesses actually needing to be ethical. Trevino and Nelson (2010) agree with this view and suggest that a perception that an organisation is behaving well will increase its attractiveness and thereby its stakeholder commitment.

On a more theoretical level, Svensson and Wood (2008) offer a model that shows how business and society are mutually dependent, and that both are responsible for the consequences and effects of the other as part of a dynamic two-way process. Crucially, Svensson and Wood also demonstrate that the ethical standards of business stem from those of society. Interestingly, most major religions also have something to say about how businesses should conduct themselves in society. Sharia banking law prohibits charging interest on loans, Confucian thought discourages profit-seeking, and Christianity has the fundamental principle of treating others as you would have them treat you. Businesses then, are not isolated from society, and the examples given above illustrate that the idea of businesses being 'value-neutral', and the argument that they can release themselves from social mores, do not hold true.

To me the most obvious proof that businesses are part of society is that their activities have social consequences. This fact has become even more of a concern over the last few decades, as the size, globality and political power of corporations (including finance corporations) have increased. An excellent example of the profound consequences unethical business behaviour can have (and indeed of all the arguments for business ethics I have given so far) is the US financial crisis of 2008. Here, four main factors combined to create global financial chaos: banks behaving unethically to borrowers (lending money they knew the borrowers could not repay) and creating unethical financial products (credit default swapping); an overly lax attitude from credit rating agencies; unethical regulatory practices (particularly the repeal of the Glass Steagall Act); and finally, 'ethical blindness' from boards of directors and risk assessors within the banks themselves (PSI 2011). The chaos that ensued not only affected the USA, but caused a global lack of confidence in the financial markets and helped hasten the European sovereign debt crisis. Whether you believe that such crashes are an inherent part of free-market economics (as proposed in the European Commission's 2009 report) or that the unethical behaviour of the banks caused an atypical financial crisis (as suggested in the US Senate sub-committee report (PSI 2011)), the 2008 crash had legal but nevertheless highly unethical business behaviour at its core.

My third and final reason for stating that business ethics is important is as a tool for analysis, research, study and education. As shown above, the power of organisations is increasing both nationally and globally, and the decisions business people make can have far-reaching effects. Despite this fact, managers surprisingly often have no specific training in ethics. I would argue that events such as the 2008 crash outlined above demonstrate that such training is needed, and that business ethics as a field of education and training within organisations is vital. The study of business ethics is also important because it provides an informed framework and source of criteria through which business behaviour can be analysed and evaluated by legal bodies and other groups in society. As Crouch (2011) states when discussing the political and financial power of multinational corporations, civic society now has a crucial role in analysing how these businesses behave and in criticising them and voicing concerns. Even if particular behaviour is legal at the time of an event, analysis of the activity and its impact in terms of agreed ethical standards, can lead to modified or new legislation.

To answer our two initial questions of whether ethical business behaviour is important and whether business ethics is valid as an area of study, I have shown that the answer to both questions is yes. I would go even further and state that globalisation means that business ethics is now much more significant than in previous eras. It's true that although a business needs to be seen as ethical, we cannot assume that it really is behaving ethically, and even if it is, this may be a result of a strategy aimed at profit rather than moral conduct. Nevertheless, pressures such as public reputation, auditing and recent legislation on corporate responsibility, mean that businesses are being forced to act more ethically whatever the personal motivation of managers. I have also argued that in fact, the long term success of a business requires a level of ethical conduct, both internally and with external clients. Most importantly, I have shown that businesses are part of society and that they should therefore adhere to the same moral principles, and I have used the 2008 financial collapse as an example of what can happen to society when businesses act unethically. As Trevino and Nelson (2010) state: 'Ethics is not just about the connection we have to other beings – we are all connected; rather, it's about the quality of that connection' (p. 32). I have shown that this is as true in the business context as in any other.

References

Carr, A. Z. (1968) 'Is business bluffing ethical?' *Harvard Business Review*, 46(1), pp. 143–153.

Collins, J.W. (1994) 'Is business ethics an oxymoron?' *Business Horizons* 37(5), pp. 1-8.

Crane, A. and Matten, D. (2010) *Business Ethics* (3rd edn.). New York: Oxford University Press.

Crouch, C. (2011) *The Strange Non-Death of Neoliberalism.* Cambridge: Polity Press.

European Commission; Directorate General for Economic Affairs (2009) *Economic Crisis in Europe: Causes, Consequences and Responses*, European Economy, 7. Luxemburg: Office for Official Publications of the European communities. http://ec.europa.eu/economy_finance/publications/publication 15887_en.pdf (Accessed 15 October 2012.)

Esty, D.C. (2007) 'What Stakeholders Demand' *Harvard Business Review*, 85(10), pp. 30-34.

'Ethical Company Organisation'. Available at: http://www.ethical-company-organisation.org/ (Accessed 5 November 2012.)

Ferrel, O.C., Fraedrich, J. and Ferrell, L. (2002) *Business Ethics: Ethical Decision Making and Cases.* Boston: Houghton Mifflin Company.

Fisher, C, and Lovell, A. (2003) *Business Ethics and Values.* Harlow, Essex: Pearson Education Limited.

Fritzsche, D. J. (2005) *Business Ethics: A Global and Managerial Perspective* (2nd edn.) Boston: McGraw-Hill Irwin.

Green, R.M. (1994) *The Ethical Manager.* USA: Macmillan College Publishing Company Inc.

Prindl, R. and Prodham, B. (Eds.) (1994) *The ACT Guide to Ethical Conflicts in Finance.* Oxford: The Association of Corporate Treasurers.

Shaw, W.H. and Barry, V. (2007) *Moral Issues in Business (*10th edn.). USA: Thompson Wordsworth.

Svensson, G. and Wood, G. (2008) 'A model of business ethics' *Journal of Business Ethics,* 77, pp. 303–322.

Trevino, L.K. and Nelson, K. (2010) *Managing Business Ethics* (5th edn.) USA: J. Wiley and Sons.

'The Body Shop, Values and Campaigns'. Available at:
http://www.thebodyshop.com/_en/_ww/values-campaigns/_(Accessed 20 December 2012.)

PSI (2011) *Wall Street and the Financial Crisis: Anatomy of a Financial Collapse.* Report by the Permanent Subcommittee of Investigation, US Senate Committee on Homeland Security. April 2011. Washington DC: US Senate.
http://hsgac.senate.gov/public/-files/FinancialCrisis/FinancialCrisisReport.pdf (Accessed 30 October 2012.)

Wolf, M. (2000) 'Sleeping with the enemy'. *Financial Times,* 16 May p. 21.

Referencing styles

Below is a very brief overview of the five main referencing styles. Institutions may have their own slight variations of these different styles, particularly in the way page numbers are indicated, how brackets are used, whether book/journal titles are underlined, italicised or put in bold, and finally, whether the list of sources is called a Reference List or a Bibliography. Don't worry too much about such variations when you start your course. The key points to remember are:

- check and use the referencing guide given to you for your course;
- be consistent in the way you reference. For example, if you put book and journal titles in bold in your list of references, make sure you do this throughout and that you don't switch between bold, underline and italics;
- your tutors will not expect you to get every detail of referencing correct at first. The most important thing is to indicate clearly in your essay (not just in your list of references) whenever you have used a source in your essay, even if you make small mistakes in how you do it.

1. Harvard referencing style

This is an author and date (year) system used in many disciplines.

In your essay

Quotation

Collins (1994: 2) states that 'good ethics is synonymous with good management.'
or
Collins (1994) states that 'good ethics is synonymous with good management' (p. 2).
or
I will argue that 'good ethics is synonymous with good management' (Collins 1994 p. 2).

Paraphrase

Collins (1994) believes that you can't manage well without having good business ethics.
or
One view is that you can't manage well without having good business ethics (Collins 1994).

In your list of references[3]

(References should be listed in alphabetical order of author's family name):
Collins, J.W. 1994 'Is business ethics an oxymoron?' <u>Business Horizons</u> Vol. 37(5), pp. 1–8.

2. American Psychological Association (APA) referencing style

This is an author and date (year) system used in the social sciences. There are some small differences between the APA and Harvard system.

In your essay

Quotation

Collins (1994) states that 'good ethics is synonymous with good management' (p. 2).

Paraphrase

Collins (1994) believes that you can't manage well without having good business ethics.

In your list of references

Collins, J.W. (1994) 'Is business ethics an oxymoron?' *Business Horizons* 37(5), pp. 1–8.

3. Modern Language Association (MLA) referencing style

This is an author and page system used in the humanities and liberal arts.

In your essay

Quotation

Collins states that 'good ethics is synonymous with good management' (2).

Paraphrase

Collins (2) believes that you can't manage well without having good business ethics.

In your list of works cited

Collins, John W. (1994) 'Is business ethics an oxymoron?' <u>Business Horizons</u> 37 (5):1–8.

4. Numeric style British Standard

This is a numeric system.

---

3 The terms 'references' and 'bibliography' are sometimes used interchangeably, but strictly speaking a bibliography differs from a list of references because it includes all sources read, including those not explicitly cited in the essay.

In your essay

Quotation

Collins [1] states that 'good ethics is synonymous with good management'.

Paraphrase

Collins [1] believes that you can't manage well without having good business ethics.

In your list of references

(References are listed in numerical order, not alphabetical order.)
1. Collins J W. Is business ethics an oxymoron? *Business Horizons*, 1994, 37(5)1–8.

5. Vancouver referencing style

This is a numeric system often used in field of medicine. There are several small variations within this system so check your course referencing guidelines.

In your essay

Quotation

Collins [1] states that 'good ethics is synonymous with good management'.
or
Collins[1] states that 'good ethics is synonymous with good management'.

Paraphrase

Collins [1] believes that you can't manage well without having good business ethics.
or
Collins[1] believes that you can't manage well without having good business ethics.

In your reference list

(References are listed in numerical order, not alphabetical order.)
1. Collins J W. Is business ethics an oxymoron? *Business Horizons* 1994; 37 (5):1–8.

6. Chicago / Turabian referencing style

This is a numeric system.

In your essay

Collins[1] states that 'good ethics is synonymous with good management.'

In your footnotes

1. John W. Collins, 'Is business ethics an oxymoron?' *Business Horizons* (1994): 37(5), pp. 1–8.

Abbreviations and labels used in dictionary entries

Meaning of abbreviations used in dictionary entries

For an explanation of the different word classes, see Appendix 6 below.

adj. = adjective
adv. = adverb
conj. = conjunction (a word that joins two clauses)
intr. or *intrans.* = intransitive verb
This is a verb that does not take a direct object (and so also has no passive form). For example: 'The sun rises.'
Note that there are some verbs that have multi-meanings and can have both an intransitive and transitive form, for example, the verb *conclude*.
(intr.) 'Oswald concluded that there was no direct link between wealth and happiness.'
(trans.) 'I will conclude **the essay** with a discussion of the implications.'
mod. = modifier.
This is a noun used as an adjective to modify a second noun. For example: 'a **family** reunion'.
n. = noun
pl. = plural noun
prep. = preposition
sing. = a singular noun or a noun treated as singular. For example: '**Genetics is** an interesting field of study.'
tr. or *trans.* = transitive verb
This is a verb that needs a **direct object**. For example: 'Table 1 shows **our data**.'
Note that there are some verbs that have multi-meanings and can have both an intransitive and transitive form. (See under *intr.* above.)
usu. = usually used as
v. = verb

Registers labels used in dictionary entries

The word *register* when referring to language, means the commonly accepted style and level of formality of language used in a particular context. For example, medical staff use a medical register when talking to each other in a professional setting.

Register labels used in dictionary entries which indicate that the word is suitable to use in an essay are: *formal / form.* and *technical.* If no register label is given for a word, it is probably suitable to use in an essay.

Register labels which indicate that the word is <u>not</u> suitable for essays are: *Informal / inf., dated, archaic, poetic/literary, rare, humorous, euphemistic, dialect, offensive, vulgar, slang, derogatory.*

A brief explanation of word class

Note that some words can belong to more than one word class depending on how they are used.

For example: 'The government will **debate** the motion next week.' Debate used as a verb.

'There has been a great deal of **debate** on the ethics of cloning.' Debate used as a noun.

Noun (n.)

A noun is a thing, place or person. Proper nouns are names of specific people or places, and abstract nouns (for example, *happiness* and *economics*) are nouns that you can't actually see or touch. Some nouns are uncountable / mass nouns (for example *evidence*, *information* and *importance*) and are used in the singular form only. To talk about an uncountable noun in the plural you need to add another noun that indicates the plural aspect.

Uncountable noun	Incorrect use	Examples of correct use
evidence	the evidences are	the different types of evidence are
information	several informations	several pieces of information
importance	several importances	several important aspects

Verb (v.)

A verb is an action, event or state. The verbs *be*, *do* and *have* can be used on their own as a main verb or as a supporting (auxiliary) verb together with a main verb. As supporting verbs, *be*, *do* and *have* indicate either time, a negative or a question.

be, do, have as a **main verb**	**be, do, have** as a supporting/auxiliary verb + *main verb*
I **am** happy. I **was** happy.	I **am** *studying* journalism
I **do** the same thing every day.	**Do** you **want** the job? I **don't** *want* the job.
I **have** a car.	I **haven't** *seen* the film.

The verbs *will, shall, can, could, may, might, must, should, ought to* and *would*, (and the phrases *to be able to, to need to* and *to have to*) are always used as supporting verbs with a second main verb to express possibility, request, necessity, certainty or caution.

These verbs are called modal or modal auxiliary verbs. They are called modal verbs because they indicate the 'mood' of the main verb.

Modal verb + *main verb*

We **should** *consider* all aspects of the issue. The data suggest that there **might** *be* a link.

Adjective (adj.)

Adjectives describe a characteristic or quality of a noun. For example: 'It is an **arguable** issue.'

Some adjectives have a comparative and a superlative form. For example: large, larger, largest.

Adverb (adv.)

Adverbs give more information about a verb, adjective or another adverb.

An **adverb** describing a *verb*: 'The economy *improved* **slowly**.'
An **adverb** describing an *adjective*: 'It is **arguably** an *important* issue.'
An **adverb** describing another *adverb*: 'We added the liquid **very** *carefully*.'

Preposition (prep.)

Prepositions describe the time or space relationship between things.

Examples of prepositions are *in, at, on, of, to, with, over, under, between, through, during, before, after*. Note that the word *to* is usually used as a preposition ('She went to the conference.') but is also used to indicate the infinitive of a verb (e.g. *to discuss*) and has one use as an adverb ('She pulled the window to before going to sleep.').

Conjunction (conj.)

Conjunctions link phrases or clauses within a sentence or link separate sentences, showing the logical relationship between them. Examples of conjunctions are *and, in addition, also, moreover, but, either... or, both... and, not only... but also, however, nevertheless, despite, after, before, since, while, until*. Some words such as *after, before, as, since* and *until* can also be used as prepositions.

Pronoun (pron.)

Pronouns replace full nouns. A pronoun usually refers to a full noun or noun phrase that precedes it.

The subject pronouns are *I, you, he, she, it, we* and *they*.

For example: '*The diagrams* in the text distract the reader from the main argument and **they** also overcomplicate the issue.'

The object pronouns are *me, you, him, her, it, us* and *them*.

For example: 'Our results indicate that *job satisfaction* is less important for new employees. **It** also seems to be less important for part-time employees.'

The possessive pronouns are *mine, yours, his, hers, its, ours* and *theirs* and *whose.*

For example: '*This book* is **mine**.'

The reflexive pronouns are *myself, yourself, himself, herself, itself, oneself, ourselves, yourselves,* and *themselves.*

For example: 'Virginia Woolf thought of **herself** as a writer from an early age.'

Note that pronouns are useful for linking ideas and sentences and for avoiding repetition. However, a common error is to use pronouns where it is unclear what they refer to because the preceding clause or sentence has more than one subject or object.

For example: 'Smith disagrees with Wolf on the issue of business ethics. **He** states that . . .'

This sentence is unclear because we are not sure whether *he* refers to Smith or to Wolf. A clearer sentence would be: 'Smith disagrees with Wolf on the issue of business ethics. Wolf states that... '

Determiner (det.)

Determiners give more information about a noun. There are four types of determiners:

Articles

A, an and *the*

Demonstratives

This, these, that and *those*
Demonstratives can be used in a similar way to pronouns, but unlike pronouns, you can also use a determiner and noun together to make your meaning more clear.

For example: 'At the conference, representatives from the six countries had a heated debate about how to balance economic development with sustainable use of resources. **This** is causing increasing controversy across the globe.'

In this sentence it is unclear whether *this* refers to the conference, to the heated debate, or to the issue of balancing development and use of resources. A clearer sentence would be: 'At the conference, representatives from the six countries had a heated debate about how to balance economic development with sustainable use of resources. **This issue** is causing increasing controversy across the globe.

Possessive determiners (also called possessive adjectives)

My, your, his, her, its, our and *their.* These are not pronouns because they do not replace a noun but are used with one.

For example: 'This thesis is interesting.'

Note that *his* can also function as a possessive pronoun and that *her* can also function as an object pronoun (see above).

Quantifiers

These are words such as *all, some, each, every, few, several, many* and *most.*

Index of vocabulary given in Part B

Subject index

Printed in China